ALSO PUBLISHED BY TRANSGRESS PRESS

Love Always:

Partners of Trans People on Intimacy, Challenge, and Resilience

Edited by Jordon Johnson and Becky Garrison

Queer Rock Love: A Family Memoir

Paige Schilt

Real Talk for Teens:

Jump-Start Guide to Gender Transitioning and Beyond

Seth Jamison Rainess

Now What?

A Handbook for Families with Transgender Children

Rex Butt

New Girl Blues. . .or Pinks

Mary Degroat Ross

Letters for My Sisters: Transitional Wisdom in Retrospect

Edited by Andrea James and Deanne Thornton

Manning Up: Transsexual Men on

Finding Brotherhood, Family and Themselves

Edited by Zander Keig and Mitch Kellaway

Hung Jury: Testimonies of Genital Surgery by Transsexual Men

Edited by Trystan Theosophus Cotten

Giving It Raw: Nearly 30 Years with AIDS

Francisco Ibañez-Carrasco

Life Beyond My Body

Life Beyond My Body
A Transgender Journey to Manhood in China

Lei Ming
with Lura Frazey

First published 2016 by Transgress Press

Library of Congress Cataloguing in Publication Data

Life Beyond My Body: A Transgender Journey to Manhood in China / written by Lei Ming with Lura Frazey

ISBN 10: 0-9860844-8-4

ISBN 13: 978-0-9860844-8-5

Transgress Press, Oakland, CA

Acknowledgements

Foremost, I give thanks to God for bringing me to this writing journey and seeing me through it.

I would like to thank Lura Frazey. She encouraged me a lot and did an excellent job of helping me tell my story and knit the pieces of this book together.

Many thanks from Lura and me to Trystan Cotten and Transgress Press for embracing this project and paving a way for this story to be told. Your understanding of the special circumstances we brought to the table, hard work and goodwill are deeply appreciated.

We are both grateful for the support, friendship and inspiration we have received from Reverend David Weekley and Deborah Weekley, Tim Collaco and Zander Keig.

Contents

Foreword

Life Beyond My Body is a beautifully written account of heartbreak, survival, and liberation—a triumphant journey from cold, bitter hardship to the warm glow of optimism. I found Lei Ming's tale thoroughly gripping, a precious gift I felt honored to receive from a talented, brave storyteller whose origins lie in the rural landscape of a country at the intersection of ancient ways and modern technology: China.

As a Chinese American, I resonated with Lei's descriptions of his childhood as the youngest girl in a world with clearly drawn gender rules and expectations. Like the predictions surrounding my own birth at a time before ultrasounds were available, a fortune teller predicted that he would be a boy. Though my upbringing was not nearly as severe, I felt a profound kinship with the wise soul in these pages. His firsthand experience with the Chinese legacy of female subjugation and the steadfast adherence to strict gender norms are compellingly described both from the intimacy of his own victimization, and the self-awareness of a transgender man watching over his female body. As a young Chinese American trans boy growing up in the San Francisco Bay Area a generation before Lei, I often wondered if I would have survived had I been born in China. Lei Ming has given us a powerful, universal tale of survival against all odds and at tremendous risk.

Despite China's one-child policy, which took effect in 1978, Lei's family included a developmentally disabled brother, two sisters, and parents who labored long hours to support them. He describes his family as a "heap of loose sand [with] nothing to keep us together." His parents did not outwardly express affection, demonstrate concern for his well-being, or establish a sense of order with him, instead leaving him alone all day from the time he was three or four years old. Born in 1986, Lei was "as uncared for as a weed in the wind," and learned to be self-reliant in the face of hunger, injuries, and bullying. Sadly, he experienced child sexual abuse at the hands of both his brother and a neighbor, an atrocity that sometimes befalls trans and gender nonconforming young people as vulnerable members of society.

The description of Lei's family life in rural Northern China is notable for its reference to a "kang," an earthen platform used in Northern Chinese houses for heating the home, cooking, working, entertaining, and sleeping. These traditional bed stoves, which first came into use over seven thousand years ago, made the frigid climates of the north habitable. The warmth of the kang in Lei Ming's house exists in juxtaposition to the icy sense of family, a relic of the ancient practices and belief systems that permeate daily modern life in China.

Particularly striking is Lei's description of China's "barns," multiple-stall outhouses that lack plumbing or stall doors. He describes with levity the "earth-friendly properties" of an open pit that uses no running water for flushing or electricity for light. Rather than dwell on the foul odor, lack of privacy, or how creepy the barns were in the obscure night, he extols the barns for the opportunities they presented for socializing, and the ghost stories the facilities inspired.

Yet, the barns, with their lack of privacy, presented challenges unlike any bathroom drama that transgender Americans face. In elementary and middle school, if Lei went to the girls' side of the barn, he would get stared at and/or scare the girls. If he went to the boys' side, he would be recognized as a known girl in the boys' bathroom. Both the girls' and boys' toilets were forbidden to him. He waited all day to use the toilet until after the fifteen-minute walk home from school. But in high school, home was two hours away. The barn was available only during ten-minute breaks, with long lines of fellow students and dozens of eyes upon him as he relieved himself, which felt disconcerting. He was forced to use the barn early in the morning or late at night, and to drink very little water. As an adult, when he used the men's side, Lei had to pretend to defecate, since he was unable to stand to urinate, but the lack of visible male genitals made him feel unsafe.

His description of the barns brings a welcome international perspective on restroom access for trans people, and showcases the hardships that trans people face in underdeveloped countries, just to take care of the most basic human function that others take for granted. While transgender Americans currently fight countless "bathroom harassment" bills that threaten our right to use restrooms, Lei portrays extraordinary circumstances that are well outside of the American expectation of privacy behind stall doors.

Since homes in his village did not have indoor showers or bathtubs, bathing was a public activity that was generally off limits to him. Rather than use the public baths, he washed from a basin at home in private, only taking a bath once a year in preparation for the Lunar New Year. It could take a couple of hours to scrub off the dust that had accumulated like layers of paint over his entire body. As a university student, he was forced to use open shower facilities, which was distressing to him. Bathing was off limits to him there as well, and he stayed dirty rather than endure this naked exposure. Lei's story highlights the barriers that trans people face worldwide in order to engage in basic grooming activities that take place in public sex-segregated facilities.

Another recurrent theme in *Life Beyond My Body* is the stress Lei Ming encountered with identification documents. Without an ID that matched his gender presentation, he was unable to participate fully in society because he had to present ID when seeking employment, renting a room, and even buying a train ticket. Time after time, he faced seemingly insurmountable barriers to legal gender change, which requires gender confirmation surgery, itself difficult to access because of arbitrary protocol defined by individual surgeons and cost-prohibitive care.

In 2009, the Chinese Ministry of Health published the first guidelines for gender confirmation surgery, which are highly restrictive. One must be over the age of twenty, ask the police department for permission and not have a criminal record, have parental consent, and undergo psychiatric treatment for one year. If married, the person must ask permission from their spouse. Despite a lack of systemic support in China to live authentically without surgery, one must live in their identified gender for at least three years prior to surgery. Even if Lei managed to meet the conditions for approval, he would need the equivalent of a few years' salary to cover the costs. When Lei sought certification from a mental health provider, she assumed he was male-to-female. When he explained that he was female-to-male, she proclaimed him "incurable" and sent him away. The invisibility of transmasculine individuals amplified his burden.

Because of these barriers to changing identity documents and accessing transition-related care, Lei Ming was briefly jailed for using false identification. He describes feeling like a thieving criminal living in a sketchy underground. At one point his financial circumstances forced him to rent a small, gloomy basement room in Beijing. The beipao, poor drifters, lived in these mazes of dark basement residential compounds, while the modern buildings above ground housed the rich in bright, sunny apartments. He scrambled to make a living while marginally housed in Beijing's cold, damp underground—a fitting metaphor for his life as a trans person who was forced to circumvent China's strict laws, policies, and cultural expectations of gender.

Despite enduring a lifetime of ridicule, rejection, and isolation, Lei Ming encountered many people who appreciated him for who he was. He found spiritual connection and community among Christians who offered guidance, cherished him, and surrounded him with love. Yet he learned the hard way that some Christians could not accept him once they learned of his trans status. He questioned how to appear before the Creator. When he was genuine about who he was, he was told that he was displeasing to God and the result of sin that needed to be eradicated. He wondered if they expected him to pretend to be someone other than who he was. Suicide became alluring.

While some Christians judged him, there were others who loved him unconditionally and vowed not to disclose his trans experience. Ultimately he found happiness working as a teacher at a Christian school. This book is a true act of bravery that comes with monumental risk; most of the members of his Christian community do not know that he is trans.

There are moments of heart connection that imbue the book with optimism about the possibility of unconditional love. Lei describes beautifully the joy of falling in love with Shao Han, a fellow university student, like a "pain killer," "as if a stove was lit within me that burned away loneliness and depression." This new love with a girl who saw him for who he was, and vowed to stand with him no matter what, was like a "shining sun [that] disguised every cloud."

Once he had a girlfriend, Lei was especially motivated to find a way to access top surgery. With ingenuity and perseverance, Lei Ming was ultimately able to sidestep seemingly insurmountable barriers to access testosterone and top surgery, and live authentically as the man he always knew himself to be. His description of the joy of swimming shirtless, tempered by his panic in the river's flooding current, is a powerful image that speaks to his lifelong journey of finding body congruence, a peaceful existence, and love.

Though the relationship with Shao Han ended, Lei persevered. Despite religious persecution, systemic barriers, and a lifetime of social isolation, Lei exemplifies profound strength of the human spirit. He is truly remarkable in his determination to live authentically, and his ability to forgive those who mistreated him. Like scrubbing away the dirt that had accumulated over a year, Lei Ming strips away the layers that were necessary for his survival, and emerges clean, resilient, and triumphant, a man living with and beyond his body.

Willy Wilkinson
Author and Lambda Literary Award winner of *Born on the Edge of Race and Gender: A Voice for Cultural Competency*

Preface

A secret can be a heavy thing to bear alone. There have been so many times I have sat alone at home wishing for someone I could be open with—someone like me. In August 2013, wondering if there was another transgender Christian in the whole world who was struggling spiritually as I did, I turned to the Internet and found news of a transgender minister who had come out of the closet. In the video, the minister and his wife sat side by side holding hands. A transgender pastor and he was married! His name was Reverend David Weekley. Immediately, I tracked down his website and later sent an email, listing the questions I had always wanted to ask:

Dear Brother,

A few days ago, I searched online to see if there were any organizations for transgender Christians and I found you. How I wish I could meet you and talk to you face to face to get some emotional support. In fact, I'm far away in China, a country where transsexualism is rarely understood. Especially since I am from the countryside, my parents will never acknowledge me as a son—I'm FTM [female-to-male].

After I became a Christian in 2005, my spiritual mother kept telling me that God created me a girl and I was just living a lie. I was struggling so much I wanted to give up my faith, even my life. I survived these years and now I live in Guangzhou, where nobody knows my past. I work as a teacher in a Christian school where everybody calls me Mr. Ray, but still the loneliness and pressure of being transgender sometimes breaks me down. To hide my secrets, I can't have a close relationship with anybody.

I have only had breast surgery, two years ago, so according to the law, I can't have my gender changed on my ID. I have some questions echoing in my head all the time:

1. *Is it a sin when people cannot accept their physical body, but try to change it to fit their inner self? I'm dying to know the reason transsexuals exist. How I wish I could just be normal like everyone else. I also want to love God as others do, but I have to hide myself.*

2. *Am I asking the right thing if I pray to God to change my body or make a way for me to have surgeries, which I am not able to afford?*

3. *Is God pleased with the marriage of someone who is transgender? Can I marry a Christian woman? Will God bless our union?*

If you can reply and share your opinions, I would appreciate it very much! God bless you!

Love,

Ray

Though there was no reply, it was comforting to know that there was someone in the world who had so much in common with me, and he had gone far in life.

To my surprise, a strange, yet warmly written letter found me months later—in November of the same year. It was the webmaster of Reverend Weekley's website, writing to explain my e-mail had never been delivered to Reverend Weekley because of a technical problem that had just been discovered. This is how I came to know Lura Frazey and we struck up a correspondence.

Soon I received a reply from Reverend Weekley. He answered my questions and also made a suggestion: "Perhaps you might keep a journal or write your story for publication later. It may help other people in China to know your story when it is safe for you to share it."

The idea of writing a book was raised a second time, by Lura, in a conversation about the issue of my identification card. That was when I learned Lura was a writer. Believing her profession and her empathy for people who are transgender would make it possible for us to cooperate on this project, I decided to do it.

This book was first written in Mandarin, and then I translated it to English so Lura could help me edit it. Writing in a foreign language is like walking a tightrope. One is never sure of the steps to take. I had to resort to the dictionary every minute and would often get stuck on the translation of a phrase. In addition to the technical challenges, this book required some emotional wrestling. It took some courage to muse over my memories and my shame.

Writing my story meant opening up about vulnerabilities and private matters I'd never shared with anyone before. Now, my story is no longer simply my own. It is my gift to my LGBT family around the world.

CHAPTER 1
Who Can Give a Man His Name?

To the one who is victorious, I will give some of the hidden manna.
I will also give that person a white stone with a new name written
on it, known only to the one who receives it.

Revelations 2:17 (New International Version (NIV))

In the same way animals don't mind what people call them, I did not care what people called me when I was little. My name was merely an identifier, as everything had a name. I began to care about what I was called after I discovered my name was at odds with my inner being.

From that time on, I rejected the name printed on my identification (ID) card, which was known and remembered by my family, hometown fellows and schoolmates from kindergarten through college. Why? Because it was such a girly name and the thought of it following me for a lifetime was too upsetting.

Everyone else in my life approved of my given name, because they believed I was a girl from the moment I was born in 1986 until my graduation from university in 2008. But I knew I was a boy, and I wanted a name that suited me.

When I was about eleven-years-old, I started scouring the

dictionary for characters I would like to take as my new name. Casually and beautifully, I signed names I liked in the margins of my textbooks, sketch papers, notebooks, or any other surface I could find, during the boredom of class. Some of the names were profound, some were plain. Some lasted a long time in my heart, some a few moments. Those names were like clouds, formed and then dissipated in my own little sky. They described the self only I knew and the man I intended to become: a writer, painter, traveler, lover, husband, and father.

Those names never came to light, but that wonderful name for girls dogged me through the years of my lonely childhood, bewildered adolescence, and idle college days, on forms, test papers, certificates, and identification cards. There are a lot of gender neutral names in Chinese, but I did not propose a name change to my parents, for my original name was alright to them. Besides, I knew I was too insignificant in their eyes to warrant the trouble of going to the police office to change my name. I wasn't so silly as to imagine my parents would do that for me.

After I graduated university, I no longer had to worry that a schoolmate or friend would "helpfully" say to a new acquaintance, "Come on, don't you know Lei Jing is a girl?" As long as I didn't need to show identification, the people I met couldn't possibly know my history. Sometimes I used my real name, and sometimes I used whatever name came to my mind. Either way, I did not feel good. If I used a chosen name that I was not accustomed to, I felt like a criminal. Once, however, I was honest with a co-worker.

"A girl's name," the guy commented.

"Ah. . .yeah," I simpered.

Eventually, I started working at a school where we all used English names, and I adopted the name I use now. People rarely ask my Chinese name, but if they do and I don't have to show identification, I give my chosen Chinese name. But none of these names can be used in this book as long as I want to protect my identity.

So here, I use "Lei Jing" in place of my legal name—that wonderful name for girls. "Lei Ming," which means "thundering," shall be my chosen Chinese name. "Ray" will stand in for my English name. Although they are not the "real" names I use in daily life, it doesn't matter. I've come to understand none of these names reflect my true essence, anyway.

Abram was renamed Abraham when he was made the father of many nations. Jacob was renamed Israel, after he struggled with God and humans and overcame. Simon was renamed Peter when Jesus beheld him. What name accurately reflects my true nature? What name did God give me when he created me?

"He calls his own sheep by name and leads them out."
(John 10:3 NIV)

What name will Jesus call me? Will he call me by my wonderful name for girls as if I'm just a deranged woman?

"[B]ut rejoice that your names are written in heaven."
(Luke 10:20 NIV)

If my name is written in heaven, I hope it's not the name I was given at birth. Perhaps it will be a name known only by God, a name beyond my imagination, a name in which I will find complete belonging and assurance.

CHAPTER 2

Family Lei

Heilongjiang is a vast plain of black, fertile earth located in the northeastern province of China. The Han are the dominant nationality there and the rest of the population is comprised of Manchu, Chinese Korean, and other minorities. According to the elders, before the Japanese invasion of 1931, people lived separately there in peace among the hills, forests and fields of what was, at the time, Manchuria. The Japanese occupation drove the Chinese out of their homes and forced them to live packed together in a certain region, and that was the beginning of my hometown.

Rice and corn fields extend to the foothills surrounding the town. A river, clear as a virgin's conscience, flows gently through the hills from east to west across the southern part of town. A white stone bridge connects the two banks. People rarely know or ask where the source of the river is or where it is heading, as they rarely know or ask where they are actually from or where they are going. They live a self-sufficient life by raising vegetables, fruit trees, poultry, pigs, horses and cows in their yards, which are fenced by timbers. The Family Lei live in this village by the river in the southwest part of the town.

Lei Limin is my father. In 1970, three years after the birth of his first child, a son was born to his family. Life seemed happy and quiet for the twenty-five -year-old carpenter with a wife, a daughter and a son. From time to time, he traveled to other places to work. Anticipating Limin's return home, his wife would stand at the crossing with her son on her back, watching for her husband's return.

When the boy was three-years-old, Limin's absence lasted much longer than usual. Day after day, his wife waited for him, gazing anxiously at the end of the road, hoping his figure would eventually appear, but she never saw him.

Maybe rumors flew to her ears, saying her dissolute husband was spending time with another woman, so doubt, anger, fear and desperation eventually overtook her. Some people said she was mentally deranged

She committed suicide by taking pesticide on a quiet night broken only by the crying of her children and dogs barking. Alarmed by the noise, neighbors rushed to the scene to find her on the ground in spasms and near death, her horrified, wide-open eyes full of pain and regret. Maybe she saw the pit of hell swallowing her, the unquenchable fire consuming her, and that was much more real and horrible than the thought of being abandoned by her husband. By the time she realized what a silly thing she had done, it was too late. Finally, her spirit departed, leaving a hard, cold corpse for her husband to bury.

Soon after, several young women were introduced to Lei Limin, who was known for his intelligence and skill. His father was also the chief of the marketing cooperative of the town, which was a noteworthy position at the time. Limin was content with the second daughter of the Family Su, who lived in the north.

Su Yanchun was an innocent, twenty-two-year-old girl, tall, healthy and good looking, with two black braids. She had never been in any love affair before and hadn't a clue about marriage.

What would it mean to marry a man whose wife just committed suicide leaving two children behind? What impact would this have on Yanchun and her own children? Would she be able to bear it? Yanchun didn't give a lot of thought to these things. Maybe people said it was time for her to get married and she felt compelled by tradition. I suspect it didn't matter to her who she would marry. She just followed convention at the approval of her parents. A farmer's daughter who had survived great famine, living in a society upended by the Cultural Revolution during her adolescence, Yanchun had probably never heard of any other path for her life.

Neither did Limin know, nor feel the need to know, what kind of person his new wife was. Marriage, for him, was nothing more than spending days and sleeping together. He did not consider whether they would get along well, or even if this woman was competent to be a step-mother to his children.

Thus, two foreign souls were bound together. I believe their souls are still strangers, even today.

Yanchun was not a woman who treasured herself much, nor did her husband care for her. So, she worked hard every day, even when she was heavily pregnant. While chopping and binding firewood in the yard, she miscarried her first child. It was a boy.

In time, Yanchun became pregnant again. One day, she was resting on the *kang*—a heatable brick bed used in northern China—when Limin asked her to wash the dishes. While she was trying to get off the kang, Yanchun slipped, fell down, and miscarried her second boy. Limin would regret that moment forever.

In the meantime, the son born to Limin's first wife was found to be physically and mentally disabled. One of the boy's legs did not grow as long as the other and his foot shriveled. He wet the bed until his twenties. He couldn't speak properly or pronounce words clearly, so people hardly understood what he said. Nor, did he look anyone straight on, but peeked, showing only the whites of his eyes. He acted like a thief trying to hide the things he did, afraid to be discovered. When confronted, he always denied what he'd done.

The boy had a decent name, but it was almost forgotten. Limin and Yanchun called him "Idiot." Some people in the village called him "Dumb," while those who were friendly called him "Boy." A room in the corner of the house was assigned to Boy. He lived alone, and the door was closed all year round.

Wanting a healthy son, Limin was pleased when Yanchun became pregnant again and did not miscarry. In 1976, their first child together was born: a daughter. Four years later, despite the large sum of money they would be fined—China's One Child Policy was implemented in 1978—they had a second child. A girl again.

Another pregnancy was attempted. B-mode ultrasound wasn't available yet, so Limin had to gamble. He went to a fortune teller who predicted the baby would be a boy, according to the time the child was conceived.

In March 1986, the crying of a newborn in Lei's house broke the dawn. Seeing no penis between the baby's legs, Limin's excitement faded to disappointment. One more girl was the last thing he wanted. He gave up.

No one knew that day, or for years to come, that Limin's youngest child was actually a boy. They named me Lei Jing.

Family is where we start the journey of life, where we are nurtured and connected with the world after birth, and where our self-portrait is first formed. But sometimes, the family that should bring us happiness is a source of pain. Those that should have drawn us in, drive us out.

"Couple" is supposed to be a synonym for intimacy and love, but Limin and Yanchun were aloof toward each other. Though legally married, they never hold hands, never hug, never pat, never gaze into each other's eyes, never appreciate, never call each other "darling." When one needs to get the other's attention, they simply say, "Hey!" as if it is shameful to call the other's given name. Chinese people of their age tend to be reserved anyway, especially in rural areas. Beyond that, neither has a warm personality. Limin is a silent man who rarely communicates or expresses much. Yanchun doesn't know how to please her husband; nor is she fond of children. As a girl, she preferred working with her mother in the hills over caring for her younger brothers and sisters. As an adult, she preferred working all day long to nurturing her young—or maybe she had no choice.

After her marriage, Yanchun needed a way to make a living. Limin's wages were insufficient to support their growing family. As the primary cook in the Lei household, Limin stocked the cupboards with rice, oil, fruit, snacks and other groceries. He also kept a vegetable garden, which flourished under his hand. But, school fees and books still had to be covered, and that responsibility fell to Yanchun.

She taught herself to be a tailor by studying books. Fear drove her to work day and night, because her husband would not give her money. While she toiled to ensure their future, her children shifted for themselves.

By the time I was born, the oldest daughter of Lei had already moved away from home and was working in Daqing. She would eventually move to Shandong province, marry, and have a good life. She seldom came back to visit her hometown. The middle daughters, Lei Yun and Lei Lan, were in school. I was fed milk powder instead of mother's milk and sent to my maternal Grandmother's, or sometimes, a neighbor's house while Yanchun worked.

Because I rarely saw my parents during the first several years of my life, I didn't know which family I actually belonged to. People made fun of me by asking, "Tell us, Jing, whose family are you of?"

Proudly, I would say, "I'm Family Liu's!" Then everyone would burst out laughing.

Bewildered, I would ask, "What's wrong?"

For a long time, I thought Auntie Liu was my mother. Even if I slept with my own family, I would run to Auntie Liu's home when I woke in the night. I had no memory of my real mother's embrace or my father speaking to me with tender eyes or gentle words. Dad and Mom were no more than people who never stayed at home in the daytime.

In the mornings, Dad got up first and cooked—usually a pot of soup. The food was mainly bean curd, potato, spinach, cabbage, radish, carrot and so on. Whoever woke up and got ready, just came to the table, ate alone and then left without saying a word. As Dad was cooking, Boy would crack open his door and reach a dark, shaking hand to the round dinner table just outside his room. Pressing on the table to balance his body, Boy moved out slowly. A red, dirty pail with a lid would come into sight, hanging from his other hand. Then, he would limp through a narrow passageway to the main door with one of his feet dragging along the floor, and the unique rhythm of his footsteps echoing around the room. He would hobble by the front windows to the backyard and dump his urinal into the pit. Next, he would wash his face, leaving behind mud drops on the bar of soap, and make his way to the table. There he would sit, looking abashed and showing the whites of his eyes from time to time, as he waited for breakfast to be ready. When he finished eating, he would drop his chopsticks and begin his day of wandering.

Mom usually got up after Dad left for work and Sisters headed to school. For a little while, Mom would sit in a trance with the quilt piled on her crossed legs. Then she would slowly dress, roll the quilt, and get off the kang. After a visit to the toilet, she would turn the bedroom into a dusty workshop again. The kang, which doubled as her work stand, would soon be covered with patterns and strips of waste cloth in various colors. First, she would press the pants or jackets she had made the night before. The room would fill with the sound of steam spray and the smell of ironed cloth. Sometimes she hummed to kill the boredom, other times she worked quietly, and occasionally, she complained tearfully. She might moan because her mother-in-law accused her of not doing any housework, but she had one hundred and one reasons to feel wronged. The main cause of her bitterness was her husband's disloyalty and irresponsibility. Often, when the children came to her in need of fees for school, she responded fiercely, "Go to your Dad!"

But Dad would say, "Go to your Mom!"

In the presence of her kids, Yanchun wept about how hard she worked to support the family and pay the tuition fees, "While your damned Dad has fun outside spending lavishly on women." The whole house was soaked in her depression.

"How do you know?" I once asked.

"How do I know? Your uncle bumped into them lying in the cornfield. I'll tell you who she is. . ."

No matter how hysterical Yanchun became or how disturbing her anguish was, she swallowed her tears and worked on. After she finished pressing, Yanchun had her leisure time for the day. She would wash her face, comb her hair, look into the mirror, and apply some cheap cosmetics, unhurriedly and attentively. Sometimes she would complain about her big red nose that suffered from skin disease and carefully spread some ointment on it. Then, she would sit alone, eating rice and cold soup from the bowl her husband had already used for his breakfast. Finally, she would set out from home carrying a big black bag full of clothes for customers. It was a 15 minute walk to her shop in town. She would not return until sunset, and most days she skipped lunch. From season to season, year after year, Yanchun was like a machine that could never stop—not even for her children.

Our family was like a heap of loose sand, there was nothing to keep us together. Supper was the only time we even sat together. Once we finished eating, we separated and the house was full of noises: television, the sewing machine, and Dad snoring. But supper didn't always happen. Dad had to travel sometimes, Mom worked late at her shop, and my sisters were rarely home. If they weren't at high school or working, they were at my paternal Grandmother's house, since our kang was too small to provide sleeping space for everyone.

Because of how my family was, I didn't learn discipline or a sense of order as a child. I never called my older sisters "*jiejie*," as younger sisters are supposed to do. I used their given names, or a nickname like my parents did, until I was older and learned it was actually impolite and uncommon for younger children to address older children that way in a Chinese family. Of course, my sisters never called me "*meimei*," or "Younger Sister," either.

Starting around the age of three or four, I was left at home all day. My only company was the tick-tock-tick-tock black clock, a big gentle dog, and Boy, who seldom stayed at home either. He wandered around town all day long, only coming back for a drink, a meal or a place to sleep.

Sometimes I followed Boy. The two of us would stagger about until we came to our father's mother's house on the other side of the village. There we stood before Grandma: a dirty kid with a runny nose and rumpled hair alongside a disabled boy, both leaning against her door frame without stepping in or saying anything. The sight of us made Grandma uncomfortable and disgusted. She would give us some biscuits from her cupboard and send us away like beggars.

Usually as uncared for as a weed in the wind, I learned to take my chances in the world. No one prevented my recklessness or showed concern when there were obvious consequences.

Once, I was walking across a frozen pond and fell through the ice. A young man passing by saw what happened and pulled me out. I walked home by myself, removed my cotton-padded pants, and lay down in my quilt on the kang. Though I called for someone to come and check on me, my family was watching TV and nobody responded. Another time, I injured my foot and had trouble walking for the rest of summer vacation, but my parents never said a word. That's how it was. If I got myself into scrapes, I had to get myself out. When I got hurt, I did the best I could to bind my wounds. If I felt ill, I found some random white pills and took them with cold water, though they usually just made me feel worse. No one seemed to notice me.

Alone at home in the afternoons, I sometimes worried that an accident had happened to my family, preventing their return. Despite their neglect, I loved my parents, as every child does. The lower the sun dipped in the sky, the more I fretted, wondering if they were alright. I was terrified they would die.

One stormy day, when I was about six and home alone, the sky and the room turned appallingly murky. Lightening flashed fiercely, illuminating the walls. The windows trembled every time it thundered. Rain poured down, forming a river in the yard. The trees swayed forcefully and fruits were blown all over the ground. It was as if heaven was in a fury to punish those bogeymen in the folktales. I felt every clap of thunder reverberate right above my head. Quaking and shrinking in a corner, I knelt down to pray.

"God of heaven, protect my mom, have mercy on my mom, please. I don't know if Mom has an umbrella with her or not."

Finally, Mother arrived home, but she did not ask if I was alright or how I had fared alone. She never showed any concern about how I was.

Another evening, at dusk, I was bored and playing by myself in front of the house gate. Finally, Lei Lan, who was in middle school by that time, appeared at the turn of the lane, dragging her tired feet, her heavy school bag over one shoulder. She looked so low I ran to her and followed her to the house. There was no food. Lan cast aside her school bag and went straight to bed. When I crawled in beside her, she said, "It seems Mom takes care of nothing except paying for school." We lay in the dark together, famished, and fell asleep with our clothes on.

Like everyone who lived in that house, Lei Lan wanted out. An excellent student, she managed to scrape her way into the best high school in the county and, years later, a renowned university. She eventually went to a big city in the south, married there, and never came back.

In my family, the one beam of light that penetrated the cold was my sister, Lei Yun. She gave me the only love, care and warmth I had in those days. She was the little mother of our family. She cooked when our parents were absent, washed everyone's clothes, tidied the house, and took care of her younger siblings. Since she was not very good at her studies, she worked after high school. Her jobs were modest: salesperson, waitress, barber or factory worker. But despite her low income, she spent generously on clothes, gifts and essential things for me that my parents never bought.

Sister Yun once had a love affair with a playboy she met in the county where she worked during her early twenties. For a time, Yun and her paramour lived with our family. One day, I was unhappy with something Yun's boyfriend did. I said something offensive in retaliation. The boyfriend, an irritable man, picked up the first thing that came to hand—the television remote—and flung it right at my head. Then, he jumped up and came after me, intending to hit me. Seeing this, Yun rushed over and stopped her boyfriend from harming me. He slapped Yun and then swept through the house as fast as a whirlwind collecting his belongings and ran into the night. Disregarding her own pain and the trouble in her romance, Yun turned to me immediately. She rubbed my brow ridge where the TV remote had hit me and took me into her arms.

Tearfully, Yun asked, "Are you okay? Does it hurt?"

I'm touched whenever I recall this and grateful to have her as my sister.

The indifference of everyone else in my family confused and hurt me. I couldn't understand why I mattered so little to them.

CHAPTER 3

Odd Boy Out

Traditionally, a celebration is held when a Chinese baby is one hundred days old, and a picture is taken of the baby as a keepsake. When I was young, especially in the countryside, cameras were rare and having portraits made was a matter people took seriously. I do not have a one-hundred-days picture. Maybe my parents forgot about it. The earliest photograph of me was taken when I was one thousand days old.

In this one-thousand-days picture, a homely little child stands stiffly on a grassy river bank. In a homemade sheer green shirt with short sleeves, blue-dotted white shorts and plastic sandals, the child looks stout and dark from sunburn. I can imagine how he or she gives off a smell of earth. A small green crabapple, fresh-picked and half-eaten, is in one hand. The child's hair is short and sticking up. Below this, thick eyebrows frown. The child looks a little confused and bothered, as if wondering what is going on—as if there are questions he or she wants to ask, but is too young to know how to express. As for the child's gender, a stranger would most likely see a boy.

In the next picture taken of me, I would be identified as a girl. I vaguely remember the day it was made. I was in my maternal grandmother's house. Grandma combed my hair, braided it, and fitted me with a headdress flower. She dressed and groomed herself well, too. My sister, Lei Yun, arrived on her bike and Grandma collected another granddaughter on the way to the photography studio.

In this picture, a little girl in red pants and a milky vest holds an artificial flower. Next to her is an amiable elder woman who is seated. Two older girls stand behind Grandmother. The littlest girl tilts her head to one side, looking somewhere else. She is in the scene, yet remote from what is happening.

I guess I was about four that day. If I did not have this picture as proof, I would have never known I once looked like such a clean, pretty girl.

Who could have known that little girl would grow up to be a man? Why did that happen? Was she born to be that way, or was there some other cause? How I would like to go back to those innocent days and investigate—to go back to my mother's womb and examine what happened to cause my transsexualism. Was it predestined by my Creator? Or, as some people say, the consequence of environmental factors or human error? Little Baby, do you know if you are a girl or a boy? Eventually, you will have to take a stand on one side or the other. All your life you will know yourself to be a son, a brother, a husband, a father—a man—yet the people who see your body will believe you to be a woman and presume you a daughter, a sister, a wife, and a mother. They will cling to their beliefs as a matter of unquestionable moral truth. You will spend decades questioning everything. Little Baby, you will come to regret and curse your birth.

Maybe it is true: happy are those who are ignorant. When I was little, I was not very conscious of gender, nor was I quite clear whether I was a girl or a boy. I was classified a girl and for a long time I believed it to be so, because that was the message projected by the outside world. But in the beginning, it seemed of no particular consequence.

Girly dressing—headwear, braids and the like—were not disturbing to me when I was very young. I was content with anything people put on me. Clothes had no special meaning to me, because I did not realize the gender-based significance of clothing. I was unconscious of hairstyles, which toilet to visit, what name I was called, what my voice sounded like, and what body parts I possessed. I never knew how to take care of my long hair: how to comb it or braid it as other girls did. One day, when I was about six, my sister cut my hair. She was about to learn hairdressing, and I was her first experiment. Since that day, I have never had long hair again.

My identified gender was not particularly stressed in the language of our home. My parents never called me "*guinv*" or "*guniang*," which means "Daughter," as other parents did to express affection. But they treated my sisters in almost the same way, and my sisters never had any trouble with their gender identity.

Because I was neglected by my parents, I was not taught to behave like a girl, nor were my boy-like behaviors restricted. My parents' behavior toward me did not reflect the gentleness associated with girls, nor the roughness ascribed to boys. It was outside our home where I discovered I did not fit in.

Xiaokai was a boy one year younger than me who lived in the lane behind my house. From the time I was four years old or so, we were together almost every day, sharing toys and food, running and climbing, rolling in straw, collecting mushrooms and leaves in the wood, exploring nature, and gleaning our first experiences about the world. We were so young no one really cared about gender, but people grow and become complex after their first few years.

The older we got, the more estranged Xiaokai and I became. He found his own friends among the circle of boys, and I was grouped with the girls. There seemed to be an invisible line drawn between us. I could not go to his side, nor could he come to mine. When I met him in the neighborhood, my impulse was to call him and run to him, but something had changed. I knew he would not accept me as his close buddy the way he had before. He would be embarrassed to be attached to a girl. Some subtle force prevented me from approaching him and left me lost, watching him from afar as he played with more socially acceptable peers. It was not Xiaokai who excluded me, but the rule of gender, which everyone took to be a fundamental law governing the systems of the world—a universal mandate we must comply with, consciously or unconsciously.

I didn't fare much better with other children. I did not know how to enter their joyous circle, so I often watched their play from the sidelines. I was fascinated by their laughing and screaming as they traveled swiftly down the playground slide. I wondered what it was like to slide down it and why it made them so excited. Look at them: apple of their parents' eyes, dressed nicely, falling over each other to climb happily to the top of the slide. I was drawn to it, too, and hesitantly stood behind the line, but I was too shy to move forward. Other boys and girls packed in front of me and slid down constantly. I could only watch the slide from afar. Eventually, I gave up and walked away, leaving the delights of the slide unknown.

Other times, I preferred to be away from the crowd, but that also set me up for ridicule. Once, in a solitary mood, I stood under the eaves of the building feeling raindrops running along my face.

"Look!" the children said, "She is like an idiot!"

Around every lonely corner, there seemed to be a new conflict.

On the first day of my second year of kindergarten, I clung coyly to Sister Yun at the door of the new classroom. Inside, I saw dads and moms settling their sons or daughters into a seat. Other parents were talking to the teacher.

"Ok, Jing, go in by yourself," said Yun, but I stuck to my ground. Seeing those adults, I felt afraid. What was I to do in there? Where was I to sit?

Teenager Yun, sent by Mom, was bashful herself, so she did not force me. We did not know what to do, so we stood there for a while and then left.

"You are good for nothing!" Mom scolded Yun when we got home, for she had failed her task.

Mother decided it was a waste of time for me to stay in kindergarten a second year anyway and my parents came up with the fantastic idea that they would send me directly to primary school by changing my age one year on the admissions paperwork.

I was led to Grade 1 by Mom, which gave me the courage to walk into the classroom full of boys and girls sitting in orderly rows. Everyone stared at me, the new classmate, as I walked to my assigned seat.

The teacher began her lesson by writing some graphemes on the blackboard. Then, she pointed at the board with a ferule and the students read aloud, following her lead. It seemed the class had already learned these graphemes a few days before my arrival, but it was a totally new lesson for me. The sound of reading ceased.

"Now I'm going to check individually," the teacher announced, running her eyes along the nervous young faces before her. The air froze. If a needle had fallen to the floor in that moment, we would have heard it.

"Lei Jing! Stand up and read!" the teacher commanded.

Although I was still lost in this new environment, the teacher's stern voice awakened me. I stood up and stared at the blackboard. I was terrified. Like a broken circuit, my mind blinked out. The teacher pointed at a letter on the board and waited. Finally, she lost her patience.

"Speak!"

I could not utter a sound.

"Like an idiot! Sit down!"

The classroom burst out in raucous laughter. Thus, I was given the label of "idiot."

Being the class idiot made me fair game for bullies on the playground. A tall girl came straight up to me where I was standing alone and, without saying a word, seized me by my collar and shook me until she got tired.

I did not understand why one child would mistreat another for no reason. Where was their hatred and violence toward me coming from? My schoolmates mocked me, called me names, threw stones at my head, and kicked me when I was walking. Often, I was afraid on the way home, wondering if some little gang would stop me and give me a hard time.

Who was that up ahead on the road? A tall girl and a little boy. Why were they walking so slowly? I hoped they were not waiting for me. I moved closer and closer, uneasily. My worry was well-founded. They each held a long stick, which they used to block my way and beat on my schoolbag.

"Please let me go!" I begged.

Just as I became desperate, wishing someone could help me, my tormentors ran away like mice accosted by a cat. I turned around, and to my surprise, there was Dad coming along the road on his bike.

It was quite unusual for me to meet my father on the road. I expected he would stop, say something comforting, and take me home. Preoccupied, he passed by without seeing me. I was disappointed, but at least he accidentally helped me escape that predicament.

School introduced practical challenges as well. At home, I could generally get away with wearing whatever I wanted. As far as I recall, my parents seldom bought me clothes. I wore hand-me-downs, mostly. Occasionally, my mother made me pants, or other garments, with leftover pieces of cloth. My family did not care what I wore as a kid, nor did I. My uncles and aunts used to mail us parcels of old clothes from their older sons and daughters. I always showed a preference for the boys' clothes they sent. I have only worn a skirt two times in my life, which is many for most men, I concede.

The first time I wore a skirt was when I was about six. My aunt bought me a pink princess skirt and conspired with Mom to force me into it.

"What a beautiful skirt!" they raved. "Put it on!"

Feeling threatened, I withdrew to a corner. "No! I don't like it!"

"Why not? See how beautiful it is?" They couldn't understand why I did not like the skirt.

The battle lasted for a while. Finally, I gave in and they put it on me. They were happy and satisfied, but I felt constrained and uncomfortable. The texture and smell of the lace made me feel ill. Immediately, I took it off and ran away.

The matter of clothes was more complicated outside the house. I was about nine the second and last time I wore a skirt. It was for an important sports tournament in my town. I was lucky to be chosen as something like a standard-bearer who walked in front of a team holding a sign. All the standard-bearers were girls. We were required to wear a white blouse and a skirt of any color. I could not escape. Gnashing my teeth, I put on a yellow skirt of my sister's, but a boys' style shirt. The moment it was over, I rushed home and changed back into my shorts, which had been handed down from a male cousin.

From time to time, my family would try to pressure me into wearing girls' clothes to school, but the only time they succeeded was once in Grade 3. My class was going on a field trip that day. Mom and Lei Lan decided I was going to wear girls' pants.

"If you don't wear those red checked pants, we will not let you go to the field trip," they said.

Field trips are big events to kids, like important festivals. There was no way I was willing to miss it, so I capitulated. I felt uneasy the whole day and changed back into my gray pants the minute I got home.

My insistence on wearing boys' clothing earned me continuous taunts and scolding from my mother. At school, it reinforced my position as a laughingstock.

In China we celebrate Children's Day on June 1st. In honor of the occasion, there are performances, games, and so forth, at the primary schools. I got up early the morning of Children's Day and put on my white shirt, blue pants, and red scarf—the boys' costume—to perform in my class chorus during the show. Sure enough, when I got to school, everybody laughed at me, including the teacher. But, I'd preferred being laughed at to putting on the girls' costume. Happily,

I managed to blend in with the boys on the stage. As a seven-year-old kid, I could do this, and people would just laugh it away.

Toilets were another issue that cropped up after I started school. In my primary, secondary and high schools, the toilet was built outdoors at a corner, above a ditch. From outside, the toilets looked like a barn built with red brick walls, a cross-shaped air vent, and asbestos tiled roofs.

A good sense of humor is useful any time a barn toilet is one's only option. If you ever have the opportunity to use one, try divorcing yourself from reality. Rather than dwelling on the open pit beneath you, focus on its Earth-friendly properties: no water is wasted by flushing and it is illuminated only by sunlight, so it costs no electricity. If you are in favor of a strong economy, you may appreciate how barns provide honest, though vile, work for the people who clear the pits. Social butterflies might prefer the barn to private facilities. Since there are no stall doors, it is very convenient for chatting with friends. Even conversations over the walls can be heard clearly. The imaginative will find the experience exhilarating. Especially at night, the barn is a scary place, which inspires ghost stories and scandalous rumors. Tales are told of abandoned babies being thrown into the pit and indecent men standing in there, below the ladies room, peeking up. Visit the barn often enough and your own mind will likely invent similar creepy fictions for your entertainment.

Dubious advantages aside, barn toilets were a special problem for me. To start with, there was a "男" for male painted on one end of the barns and a "女" for female on the opposite side. Also, they drew a crowd despite their stink.

When I was in school, girls sometimes shared an amazing story with their friends: "You know what? I saw a guy in the toilet just now!" The guy she was talking about was me.

If I went to the ladies' room, I would be stared at and scare the girls, who would wonder: "Is that a girl or a boy? Oh my, how come a boy is in here?" If I went to the men's room, I would encounter classmates, who knew I was a "girl." Imagine the expressions on their faces. It seemed both school toilets were forbidden to me.

I envied the other boys and girls. They laughed and chased each other to the toilets at break time. I had to hold myself until I got home, which was about 15 minutes away on foot.

In our world, genders are considered opposites, as if each exists on one end of a line segment. The closer you are to one, allegedly, the farther you are from the other. If you prefer the things of one gender, you are thought to be rejecting the other. If you are absorbed in a Barbie doll, it is assumed you will ignore a Transformer. If you love girly skirts, you are expected to reject manly ties. Everyone is sure you either dream of being a wife and mother, never wanting to be a husband and father, or vice versa. In our minds, dolls, skirts, wives, and mothers are female; Transformers, ties, husbands, and fathers, are male. Does anyone think that this needs to be taught? No one I know. Moreover, we presume all this is governed by the presentation of the physical body: that a child will grow automatically to make the choices we associate with his or her genitals. I was an exception. Though I was assumed to be a girl, based on my visible body parts, I did not demonstrate the preferences or disposition usual for girls.

If there was any toy I yearned for, it was a toy gun so I could play soldier and policeman. Dad bought me a set of Transformers once, which I had pestered him about for a long time, and I treasured them. As for the activities I enjoyed, I didn't know any girls who were interested in them. I never tired of sharpening a lath into a sword or building a kite and flying it in a field. I learned to use a saw, which I loved, and sawed all the waste wood fencing into short firewood. For a time, I liked boxing, so I filled a sack of sand for practicing and hung it over the grape trellis in our yard. I even made sandbags out of waste clothing and bound them to my calves when I walked or jogged. I played with a whipping top and slingshot, did handstands and pushups, and enjoyed sports. I was up for any challenge or risk. I would jump from very high places just to see if I could, and consequently, injure my heel. I would set a goal of 400 sit-ups in one go and meet it. My love of sports toned my muscles and made my physique strong, which I was proud of.

I felt like a boy, acted like a boy and looked like a boy. However, I had the body parts of a girl and nobody else could see past that. Not that anyone would have suspected the truth. In that time and place, who had even heard the word transsexual?

CHAPTER 4

Primitive Instincts

Not all were so hostile to me. There was one smile I will never forget. In my remote memory, I can still see a nice little girl heading toward me from the school grocery. She gave me a friendly, secret smile as if she knew me. When she passed by, I must have looked like a fool, for I was stunned and melted by her unexpected kindness. Who was she? Was she smiling at me? She must be. There was no one else. I had never seen a smile so delightful and beautiful, and it was for me! Her girl's sweetness—something like sunshine—gave me a slight electric shock feeling, which was beyond my understanding. When I trace back my affection for girls, I always arrive at that smile.

I learned later the girl had just transferred to our school, and she knew we were in the same Grade 2 class. What she did not know was that she had aroused an obscure feeling in me that I was too young to name.

One Sunday afternoon a year later, I was playing with my cousin in front of my uncle's house. The daughter of a neighbor came to join us and I recognized her from the other Grade 3 class. She was Chinese Korean and had a foreign air about her. We were playing Roshambo and the loser had to carry the winner a certain number of steps.

"Paper-scissors-rock!" I lost and my new friend burst into silvery laughter. She jumped on my back and wrapped her arms around my neck without hesitation. I took off carrying her, both of us giggling happily. Inside me, the mysterious feeling first roused by a beautiful smile in Grade 2 rose and sounded, echoing so loud and clear I could not turn a deaf ear to it.

I wished I could carry her longer, if not forever. After a few steps, she jumped nimbly down and started another round of the game. The fresh scent of her sleeves lingered around my neck, preserving the sweet memory of having her on my back. My regret was immediate. If only I were a boy! Why was I not?!

To be hit by such a sweet and secret affection, was it a blessing or misfortune? A gift from heaven or a spell? Was it destined? In my blood? Or a perverted sin? Where did it come from? What was it for? Its arrival brought hope interlaced with despair.

Being born with the body of a girl was an unchangeable fact, but I was already desperate to cross that gender line. By instinct, I knew that what I felt went against convention. It was considered taboo, transgression, something impossible, never to be brought to the light, not to be divulged. But it was real and it did not wane. As I grew older, it grew too, thrived and became more intense. An intrinsic part of me, it followed me every day. I could not escape it.

My relationships with boys were similarly laden with troubling feelings. Once a new boy transferred to our Grade 3 class. He was very friendly and kind to me and happy to become my friend. I treasured this friendship and hoped he would never know the truth about me. How long could I hide on the other side of the gender line and be his peer? Not until the end of the day, as it turned out. Bodies can be covered, but that only goes so far.

When we lined up to be dismissed for home, my new friend purposely stood behind me and hugged me. Instead of feeling uneasy, as I did when girls walked arm-in-arm with me, I felt his embrace was familiar and natural. This scene caught our classmates' attention, however, and they pointed at us, laughing at my new friend for hugging a girl. To my delight, he did not seem to notice. He was caught up in the excitement of learning we were neighbors. It turned out that his family had just bought the house opposite my house and the next door down was the home of his uncle. I could not help but think of how great it would be if I was considered a boy and we could become good friends! We lived so close, and we were in the same class! It would be perfect!

We met his cousin on the way home, and she told him kindly that I was a girl. I regretted it so much.

Losing this friendship was as sad as losing my first friend, Xiaokai. My new neighbor kept his distance from me after that. Alas, how I longed to join the boys of my class when they gathered in front of his house to ride bikes together. My heart was so drawn to them, I forgot the slingshot in my hand, which I had been practicing with, and stared across the street. I felt the spirit of the boys in the air and it was also within me to be wild, reckless, masculine. But according to the rules ingrained in human culture, I did not belong with the boys.

This kind of thing happened to me once in a while. A strange boy would take me for another boy and befriend me, but reject me after he was told I was a girl. Once in middle school, a boy playing football with some other guys saw me watching from the sidelines. He waved and invited me to join them, but I pretended not to hear and slipped away. I really wanted to be friends with him, but I could not bear the loss and regret again. If I could avoid the situation, I would.

As the years passed, I became envious of other boys, which was accompanied by a feeling of inferiority to them. I was jealous of their ability to win girls' hearts and still be seen as right and proper. It galled me that I was not as tall and strong as them, and I disliked the tone they used when they talked to me—that they treated me as they did girls. All of this drove me away from boys, although inwardly, I identified with them.

However, being a top student and described as distinctive and cool, I had become popular among girls. From time to time, I would receive a letter from a girl in a different class or school asking to make friends.

To some extent, these friendships nurtured me and helped make up for the neglect I experienced at home. Sometimes the relationship would be so intimate that I had the illusion of lovers' love. My female friends gazed at me tenderly, hugged me, knit scarves for me in the cold winter, sent letters saying how much they missed me, and curled up in the same bed with me, all in the name of friendship.

Of course, I knew girls treated me this way because they took me for a girl, so these intimate acts were nothing improper to them. I felt embarrassed when they hugged me in public and got annoyed when I was called sister, but I didn't dare tell them my secret.

Girls were bewitching to me. There was one in particular when I was in Grade 8. I took every opportunity to pass by her classroom. If the door was open, I peeked inside. If I could catch sight of her, then I would be content. I tried to think of a reason to slow my steps and look at her longer. At the same time, I was afraid she would happen to look up and find me gazing at her. I had no excuse to haunt the door of her classroom, so I had to go on my way.

I dreamed I was like other boys: lively, active and free to pursue her, but of course that was just fantasy. I could only pass by her classroom again and again, faking a quick, casual glance, or look in her direction when all the classes gathered on the playground. I knew the distance between us was impassable. Still, my affection was as strong as a flood rushing against the embankment of my heart. I could not help writing a letter to her, telling her how beautiful she was. What I actually longed to say was, "I like you," but I knew I could tell her anything except that. There was no reply to such an inexplicable declaration. In her eyes, in everyone's eyes, I was only a girl dressed like a boy. Even I believed it was God's truth that the outer body infallibly represented one's gender. I was sure I could not be a boy loving a girl, certain it was all just hopeless dreaming.

One day, when I put on the new jeans Sister Yun bought me and turned to look in the mirror, the swelled shape of my hip surprised me. When did that happen? My hip had always been narrow and flat before. Some magic power was acting on my body with a will of its own. I had no control over it. This was depressing. I had no idea what other changes my body was undergoing.

Breasts budded. I felt them when I went down stairs or tried to run and was filled with shame. I adopted a heavy gait. I knew the reckless days of my childhood were gone for good. That active, aggressive boy had disappeared. My face took on a strained, melancholy expression. Gradually, I lapsed into silence and introversion.

I took to wearing an extra jacket when I went out, even in summer, to hide my changing body. Seeing me put it on, Mom would raise her head from the steaming iron in her bedroom and scold, "Are you cold? What's the matter with you? Like a fool! Who puts on a jacket in such hot weather? You just pretend to be a boy!"

Her voice! It was so piercing and derisive. In those days, it never failed to stimulate my anger. Sometimes I argued with her, but that only made things worse. Usually, I held my tongue and rushed out of the house, slamming the door, leaving her to curse me as she ironed. I would run across the bridge to the woods. There, I would weep and swear I would never go back.

I had once loved my mother very much and tried to please her or do things to lessen her burden. Her tears made my heart ache. Wanting to see her happy, I tidied up the house or presented her with my one hundred percent correct exam papers. I helped her carry the bags full of customers' clothes and learned to hem pants. I peeled oranges and apples for her; otherwise, she seldom ate fruit or had a snack. To spare her from paying book fees, I used old, borrowed text books. I thought the school report with my name ranked number one would make her proud of me, but all I received from her was an impassive face numbed by labor. Her "well done" was only a casual remark to get rid of me. Eventually, my enthusiasm to please her faded, and I learned not to invite her snubs.

"It serves you right!" or "Ne'er-do-well! You are good for nothing but costing money!" were her mantras. We seldom made physical contact. Her touch—a sudden slap on my back while she scolded me about my stoop—was so unpleasant that it provoked loathing in me. Yet, I felt guilty that I was only a burden to her.

As my adolescent consciousness awakened, bad memories of childhood swept over me. They were like tangible shadows, embittering me. If I allowed myself to think of the crimes from my childhood, they became like stones tied to me, dragging me down and down into a whirlpool of memory, intent on drowning me. Because my secrets could never be told, I had no way to relieve myself of the pain and trauma I carried. Eventually, living as a mute victim became too much. A fire of fury sparked inside me, flared up, and exploded into an inferno of rage directed toward Boy, my brother, who I was supposed to love, and who I faced every day. Unable to speak my grievances, I acted out.

Often during meals, I glared at Boy, trembling with the effort of holding back my impulses. I wanted to grab a bowl and fling it right onto his head, kick him off the stool, trample him madly on the floor, and even that wasn't enough to satisfy my pent-up anger. I hated him so intensely I wished his sudden death. Boy's chopsticks would move back and forth quickly between the plate and his mouth. His head swung a little like a duck the moment food was put in his mouth. I tried not to see him, but dipping into the same plate with him nauseated me. My appetite gone, I would drop my chopsticks and he would peep at me with the whites of his eyes.

Though I appeared quiet on the surface, I was violent and could be triggered at any time. I could not attack Boy, so I broke into his room, pulled his clothes out of the chest and threw them everywhere, dashed everything I could get my hands on, and trampled his quilt frantically, trying to relieve my hatred and fury.

I could not understand my family, and I could not understand myself. Why was I so disturbed and sad? I felt something was wrong with me. I knew I was different, but I did not know why. I did not know what I was. My inner being had never been recognized, accepted or respected.

Alone in the embrace of nature was the only place I felt free and happy. I would sit on a hillside for hours, looking into the distance, crying out sometimes. Mostly, just being myself. In the hills there were no more schoolmates to stare, ridicule or whisper, no more Mother's curse or neighbor's hateful voice. There was only the whistling of the wind in the pines. As if the hills had a spirit that received me, I sometimes lay down facing the pale sky. Then it was as if my body disappeared, my tangible existence was no more and my soul was free to merge with the spirit of the hills. All became still.

Even the sighing of the trees receded until they were more like sea waves rolling behind me.

When I stood up and looked south, layers of low hills rose and fell, pale blue and transparent as watercolor. Dots of vehicles moved slowly along a distant, winding road. What was beyond the hills? What possibilities lie there? Far down that road stood tall buildings and neon signs, which I had not yet seen. What kind of people would I meet there? Would there be hope? Happiness?

CHAPTER 5

Do You Have Testosterone?

In 2001, as the top student in my middle school, I was admitted to the best high school in the county. At last I was to leave my hometown! The bus pulled away very early one morning while the town was still quiet and sleepy. I found myself struck by nostalgia. Was that a strange feeling? Well, it was the place that had witnessed my first fifteen years. It had made a mark in my memory, which I have never escaped.

The fresh air blew through the window onto my face as the boundless rice fields slid backward in a whirl. I fell to brooding. Where was I heading? What else besides attending school? And what about after graduation? I had never thought of that, nor did I have any ideas for my future, except one: in my mind, I was a man living free from the body I had been born with.

Admission to such an excellent school is supposed to be admirable. It's supposed to mean a high chance of going to a first-rate college and getting a promising job and good prospects. The Chinese are so convinced a top high school is the certain road to prosperity that many people ensure their matriculation with bribes.

My high school brought together the top half of the most excellent students of the county. Every year, a couple of students were admitted to Tsinghua University and Peking University, which strengthened the reputation of the school. To me, the place was like a prison. Every day was exactly the same, we were forced to study subjects we might never use except during the college entrance examination, and it was crowded.

There were more than sixty students in each class and nine classes in each grade. The most was made of every classroom: desks reached to the teacher's platform and back to the wall. There never seemed to be enough air for all the lungs to breathe. Especially in winter when windows were tightly shut, one came in from the outside and noticed the smell of something stale, which was imperceptible to those who remained inside. Each half-meter desk was a battlefield where young minds fought for their future. Books piled high on desks were like fortresses, behind which, students buried their heads in exercises and tests, day and night. Competition was fierce. Students calculated their entire value as a human being based on scores achieved and class ranking. It was an investment of three years to determine one's fortune for a lifetime.

There was no time to cultivate friendships, everyone was too busy studying. From 7 am to 9:30 pm, day after day, we studied. When the dorm lights went out, studies continued in the corridor where yellow lamps were kept on. Some held their books and walked back and forth, memorizing ancient Chinese prose or political theories, some bent over stools to work math problems, some even kept their eyes fixed on a textbook when answering the call of nature. Students worked so hard they forgot time and got their days mixed up. There was no music, no art, no activities. P.E. was our only non-academic class. Every other subject we studied was for the college entrance examination. There were no expectations or surprises. Tomorrow could always be predicted; it would be a repeat of yesterday. In the beginning of my high school career, I did not share the motivation or determination of my classmates.

The crowds made me feel lost. Usually, I waited for the other students to disperse after the bell rang for break, then I would leave. I disliked moving among that throng, for I did not know where I was going, why I was there, where I was from, or why I was different from everyone else.

As usual, high school life had practical problems unique to me. Throughout primary and middle school, I had avoided the public bathrooms by holding myself until I got home. When I reached high school, home was two hours away by bus. I lived in a dormitory right behind the teaching building and had to use the school toilets as everyone else did.

When the break time bell rang, the back gate of the teaching building looked like a sluice gate that had just been opened. A flood of teenagers, full of vitality and headed for the toilets, poured through. Then they divided into two main streams: boys and girls. There were more than 1,500 students in the school. During the ten minutes allotted for break, the huge "barn" was suddenly the most popular and crowded, place on campus. Then it was my turn to be amazed at what was in the bathroom: rows of girls standing at their individual seats, many changing their sanitary towels; the sounds of tearing the sanitary towel bags; girls talking and calling out to each other; dozens of eyes upon you while you answered the call of nature. However, nobody felt awkward except me. Minutes of waiting there proved too long for me and it was disturbing to have somebody watch me, so I generally left the line before reaching a seat.

I started going very early in the morning or very late at night when there were few people. If the situation became very urgent in the day time, I asked to be excused during class or ran to the toilets as soon as the bell rang for all the students to return to their classrooms. But teachers were displeased with these behaviors, so there were times when I had to use the barn on the school's schedule.

Each phase of life falls into its own pattern and my high school life settled into a regular, boring rhythm. I visited home at the end of every month and stayed one night. The next morning, I would turn to Mother when she was ironing. She knew my intent and would give me 300 yuan, unhappily, and sometimes 50 more in a way that made me feel guilty. It was a hard moment. When would my dependence on her end? I wished I could stop costing her and repay her everything. So, I spent every penny carefully. I ate the cheapest meals, wore my sisters' clothes—although, once their clothes were on me, they looked like boys' apparel—and sometimes patched the knees of my jeans to prevent the holes from getting bigger. I knew the full weight of poverty in those years.

All these issues combined to make high school a lonely, tiresome experience. What could a stranger with few assets do to find some human companionship? I had once visited a church in my hometown as the guest of a friend. Although I did not believe God existed then, nor did I understand the message they preached, which was in Korean, I was drawn by their love. Something held them together that was beyond family bonds or friendship. They treated me kindly and seemed to watch over me, concerned about my needs. In contrast to my family, they spoke and acted gently. Remembering their fellowship, I found a church in a lane near the high school. The church was the lamp that lit my heart in those gray days. When I was weary, it was the place I would go.

Adolescent and lonely, I craved love. Eventually, I became profoundly infatuated with a Korean girl named Chun. I met her at the house of a Korean family who made their living cooking for the students of the Korean High School nearby. Introduced by a Korean friend, I started taking meals there. I met Chun several times at one table. We only had some brief conversations, but her every facial expression, act, and move left an impression on me. She was pure as a lotus, fresh as water. She sometimes wore a sheer white school suit. Other times, a light green shirt and khaki pants. Her hair might hang down, gracefully flowing, or she might tie it up and wear a white flower in it. In a word, she looked very chaste. Every time I passed her school, I looked for her figure among the boys and girls entering and leaving the gate. Though I never saw her, it became my habit to watch that gate closely. Occasionally, the sight of some girl's back in a suit similar to Chun's would warm me up. I dreamed of courting her, winning her affection, and one day, marrying her.

After a month, I had to quit taking meals at the Korean house because it was far from my school, and it cost more than other options. After that, thinking of her made me feel like crying, yet despite the ache in my throat, I laughed for the holy affection she aroused.

National Holiday came and went and it turned cold abruptly. Sparse bundles of low-headed rice made a desolate sight of the fields. Such coldness disconcerted me. I was at a loss about how to go on with this life, yet everything had to be maintained. When the bell rang, I must appear in the classroom, whether I liked it or not.

One day, I was called into the hallway and discovered my father standing at the door of my classroom. He had come to the school to attend a parent meeting. I hadn't known he was at the school. Standing there in his winter coat and padded trousers, Dad looked like a sculpture of a repairman. His hands were rough from work, there was dirt in his fingernails, and he gave forth a scent of rust. Everything about my father's appearance demonstrated to me how he toiled to support his family. It made my heart ache, and I longed for some way to connect with him.

I was so lonely and helpless, so in need of strength that would sustain me, and there I stood, face-to-face with my father, but I did not know how to reach him. I should have been able to rely on him, but I couldn't even find words. He was my father, but he was a stranger. So, I just stood there feeling like I wanted to cry.

Finally, Dad said, "I am going to catch the last bus home."

I walked with him to the school gate. Dad got onto a tri-car taxi and I watched him disappear into the night. I wished I had a family in the real sense, one that would stay by my side. The parents of some of my peers rented houses near the school to be close to their child during high school. I wanted emotional support like that, but I knew I could not expect such a thing from my parents.

In Grade 11 Biology class, we studied an experiment where scientists injected female animals with testosterone and the female animals developed male features. The teacher went on with other things, but my mind was stuck on the association between testosterone and appearing male. Testosterone? I had never heard this word before. Could this mysterious chemical work on my body too? A slight beam of hope pierced my gloomy heart.

I had not yet heard of transsexualism, but I knew it felt heavy and horrible to live in my body where female features were thriving irrepressibly. Desperately, I pressed on my breasts, hoping to prevent their development. I beat my crotch from both sides, as though it could be squeezed into its proper shape. I dreaded the attack of menses, which I knew could happen at any time. Perhaps testosterone could save me.

So, during supper break, I went out seeking testosterone. It was winter and nightfall came early, but I trudged the bleak streets past the dim lights of book shops, stationary stores, and groceries, until I saw the bright white glow of a large drugstore. I was wearing a down coat inherited from my sister, Lei Lan. Fancy Dad buying her such a masculine coat: indigo blue and dark green, puffy like bread dough swollen by yeast, good quality and very warm. It felt safe to be wrapped in that coat with my feminine hips well covered. A muffler hid my face; only my eyes were naked to the world.

"Do you have testosterone?" I asked, shyly.

"Pardon?" The saleslady looked blank.

Despite my embarrassment, I pronounced each character to make sure she heard me clearly: "Tes-tos-te-rone."

She shook her head, and so did the salespersons in other drugstores. Their expression showed they had never heard of it. Somehow, I had expected this result, but I had to try. I could not give up.

I wandered, dragging my weary legs. What kind of store might have this stuff for sale? There was a small dark building on the roadside ahead of me. Could this store have it? I paused. A high school student was not supposed to enter such a shop. The characters pasted on the window were dimly visible in the dark: SEX PRODUCTS.

I told myself it was not likely they would have testosterone for sale, but what if they did? I felt like walking away, but somehow stuck to my ground. Finally, my desire to know overcame my timidity and carried me toward that indecent wooden door for my first (and only) visit to a sex shop. I pulled the handle and walked into a small, dark room.

"Do you have testosterone?" I inquired, trying to sound calm and natural.

The man standing by the counter shook his head, perhaps

puzzled by what the strange kid in front of him was looking for. I fled immediately upon hearing his negative answer, feeling relieved, but also glad I hadn't passed up a chance, however sketchy.

For the rest of my 16th year, finding testosterone was constantly on my mind. On the bus ride home, unburdened by schoolwork and life at home, my favorite thing to do was sit by the window and let my imagination drift, stimulated by the scenes from outside. I had visions of a tall, handsome, mature man. He was a painter, strolling in a boundless field with his easel under his arm. He was a lover, embracing a girl in a wood of silver birches. He was me. I wanted to travel through life in his body.

I lived in total ignorance of what my condition was until, one day in 2003, I read the word "*yixingpi*" in a magazine article about a Chinese man who was transsexual. Suddenly, I had a word to define me. "*Yi*" means change, "*xing*" means sex, and "*pi*" means addiction. Therefore, "*yixingpi*" can be translated as "*transsexualism*" in English. To some extent, my not knowing about this condition until my third year in high school shows how poorly informed we are in my country about transsexualism. It is only in the last couple of years that the subject is being discussed more widely due to a few prominent people coming out of the closet as transgender, but I doubt anyone in my hometown has ever even heard the word "transsexual."

Learning about transsexuals was like discovering human life on another planet. One moment, I was the only person I knew like myself in the entire universe. In the next moment, I was not alone. I belonged to a group of people. I had a word to explain myself. There were others out there, somewhere, who understood what I was going through.

Immediately, I wrote to the doctor referenced in the article. Dr. Chen Huanran was a specialist. He was a leading plastic surgeon and experienced in gender confirmation surgery. For the first time, I had someone to whom I could pour out my heart. Some of my repressed secrets could finally be told. I did not have the doctor's specific address, but the article mentioned the place where he worked: Plastic Surgery Institute of Chinese Academy of Medical Sciences. Of course, I didn't actually expect my letter would find Dr. Chen. It was a long shot, but he replied!

Lei Jing,

I received and read your letter. I can quite understand your current feelings. You are still a high school student and about to take the college entrance examination. It is better for you to work hard now and make an effort to get admitted to a good university so you can receive a good education. Then we can talk about your issues.

I am enclosing my business card. If you have any questions, you may call and inquire. We can also talk face to face in Beijing if there is any opportunity for you to come.

Study hard and live positively,

Chen Huanran

I kept this letter with me for many years. It was a talisman, allowing me to touch something hopeful for my future, even if my chances were remote.

Qualifying for surgery would first require a rigorous process of psychological and physical examinations. Until 2009, there were no government laws or standards regarding gender confirmation surgery. Doctors determined their own rules and protocols, based on their personal ethics and general principles of medical care. Dr. Chen required 20 pre-conditions be met before he would perform gender confirmation surgery.

Patients had to demonstrate their desire for surgery based on an innate need, rather than external influences, and they had to prove they were not mentally ill or addicted to drugs or alcohol. The patient's next-of-kin had to attend a consultation at the hospital and the authorities had to be notified of the upcoming procedure. Dr. Chen would not operate unless the patient had graduated from university, because he felt education was critical for developing the maturity needed to handle the consequences of transition. Also, a university education helped ensure his patients could afford the high cost of surgery and would be able to support themselves after surgery. Only a small number of applicants are approved for gender confirmation surgery each year. If I was going to be among them one day, I had work to do. But, seeing a way out of my problems, my mind lit up.

In the autumn of 2003, I purchased a second-hand bike and peddled home, rather than taking the two-hour bus trip. During those long bicycle rides, I meditated on my plan. Going to a good university promised a decent job. A decent job meant a high salary, which meant the possibility of raising the large sum needed for mastectomy and genital reconstruction. It was like an adventure, for I was not sure of the way or my strength, but I told myself, "You will make it as you will surely succeed in getting admitted to a first-rate university." I pledged to go all out for the final sprint to the college entrance examinations during Grade 12.

My goal gave me new eyes for the world. Riding my bike along the main road, through villages and over bridges, I was mostly alone and free to enjoy the pleasures of nature. I did not mind the occasional bus passing by, which raised a cloud of dust. The poplar leaves were bright yellow and dazzling under the bluest sky I had ever seen. At the sides of the road, the rippling rice fields looked like a golden sea that I could not resist. I got off my bike and walked into the field. A flock of birds leaped into the air when I reached them. I sat on a ridge, resting my eyes on the landscape. I felt exhilarated. The world looked beautiful, and life seemed hopeful.

CHAPTER 6
Big Plans and Big Problems

In June 2004, Grade 12 students across the nation took the college entrance examinations and our battle was finally over. There was an emancipated atmosphere among my peers. Books that had been used as bricks to knock on the door of university had now served their purpose and were thrown out of the windows. Great packs of exercise papers were sent to the salvage station. Finally, we could chat, watch television, have a nap, daydream, and relax without feeling guilty. Those who had messed up their exams, or who were not satisfied with the results, choked back tears and braced themselves for a second try, although there were some who refused another year of that inhuman life, no matter what the consequences might be.

After about two months, I received the letter of admission from the university where I had applied. But, the tuition of 10,000 yuan per year caught me by surprise. It was normally 5,000 yuan per year. No one knew better than me how hard my mother worked. How could I live with myself if I asked for so much money?

I returned home with that honorable red letter and a heavy heart. It was dusk and they were having supper. Seeing how leaden I looked and noting I would not eat, they asked what happened.

"I want to quit school. The tuition is too much," I said, passing the envelope to them.

They read the manual sent along with the letter and were also pressured by the great sum. Mom especially, but, in a rare show of pride, my family encouraged me.

"As for the money, there must be some way," they said soothingly.

"No, I don't want to go!" I insisted, trying to subdue my sorrow.

"What's wrong? Why don't you want to go?"

I could not answer. They kept asking; I kept silent. Their voices turned loud and impatient.

"Am I not asking you? Did you hear me?" Dad demanded.

To escape his assault, I fled to the small house in our yard. My paternal grandmother had lived there in her old age. When Grandma was in residence, it was a lively house where women gathered on the heated kang and knitted sweaters, chatting and laughing away the long winter. Since she had passed away the previous year, the house had been deserted. It seemed ominous, especially at night, as if her ghost still haunted it. However, I often stayed there and enjoyed the solitude. It was my dear private space to hide.

In the little house, I sat by the window and grieved. Eighteen is an age to be celebrated and marked, an age that means independence and responsibility as a member of society, an age of flourishing youth and multicolored life. Isn't that what I hoped, persisted and fought for? My future lay before me, yet the more I longed for it, the more broken-hearted I became, for I would only be believed a female. Now, according to the university manual, an identification card would be required, which would certify that identity legally. I preferred no card at all!

The crickets sang melancholy tunes quietly in some corner. Suddenly, Mom's stout figure appeared in front of the window, which gave me a start.

"What on Earth happened? Speak, you ne'er-do-well!" she yelled.

For years she had scolded, mocked and cursed me freely as a "freak" and a "fiend." For the first and only time, I retaliated.

"You are the ne'er-do-well!" I shouted.

Hearing this, she turned away in tears and silence, feeling hurt, astounded and wronged. But how could I tell her my real problem? What could I say? Tell her I don't want identification because. . ? Could they understand? If I remained silent, they would continue.

Dad came in and turned on the light. I should have known better than to ever mention my condition to him, but desperation made me reckless.

I retrieved the magazine about Dr. Chen's case, which I kept in a drawer at my Grandmother's house, turned to the page where the story of the transsexual was reported, and presented it to him. Dad sat on the edge of the kang and started to read. I sat at a distance, wondering what his response would be. After a long silence he dropped the magazine to one side and my nightmare began.

"How damned shameless you are! As long as I am alive, don't you even dream of it! Are you not a girl? You are just pretending! I will lose face because of you! What will people say about me!" At the top of his lungs, he poured out a torrent of abuse deep into the night. "You are so addicted to this idea! You are a girl; you are not a man!" Every word was like a sharp knife piercing me.

Sobbing and choking on my tears, I was speechless, but protesting inside, "No, I am not a girl! I'm not!" How I wished I had one thousands mouths to defend myself. No one understood; no one! I was on the edge of losing my reason.

Finally, late in the night, he got tired and went to his bed. All through the night, in the small house, I lay on the kang, still and sleepless. I felt like I had lost myself and become a doll—an empty shell. My heart felt mostly dead. Only a slight impulse remained, which urged me to rush out to the bridge and dive into the water to be drowned and become a roving ghost.

By morning, Dad's temper had cooled quite a bit and he came back to the small house where I was staying.

"You know, your mom's mentality is not so good. Go apologize to her!"

Although it was disconcerting to enter that house, I obeyed.

"Mom, I'm sorry," I rumbled, bowing my head.

She raised her head from her ironing, looked at me, and said, "So you know you did wrong, huh?" Then she continued to harp: "You are a girl!" I don't remember what else she said. Maybe I closed my ears on purpose because those words were so unbearable to me.

I didn't reply. It was better to keep silent, for if I dared argue, I would only add fuel to the fire. Finally, I withdrew to Grandmother's house.

I thought I would have a quiet morning to cool down alone, but after a while, I heard footsteps approaching. Mom should have been at work at that hour, but she had returned with Aunt Zhang and a strange man, intruding on my solace.

The man turned out to be a fortune-teller. Mom believed I was demon-possessed. That explained to her why I had yelled back at her, and why I had gone insane and now claimed to be a man.

A low table was set on the kang. The man sat by it and took his professional tools out of a bag. He asked if I suffered frequent headaches or stomach aches, if I slept well, and my birthdate. He spread his lots, which to me were only a bundle of plastic strips, and asked me to draw one. I did. Apparently, I drew well. He spoke favorably according to the book that went with the lots.

Then, he asked me to pull my shirt up so my breasts were bared. I saw through his foul motive, though he posed as a decent man. Still, I did what he instructed, indifferently. I never thought of my breasts as part of my body anyway. He dipped a writing brush in red ink and drew circles around my nipples while Mom and Aunt Zhang watched approvingly from one side. Then he wrote some inscrutable symbols in red on a strip of yellow paper. He rolled an egg—believed to bring good fortune and exorcise evil spirits—over the writing, then set the egg aside and folded the paper. Finally, he sewed the paper inside a pouch of red cloth, which he pinned under the arm of my shirt.

Despite my compliance, I had not given up resisting internally. I hadn't forsaken myself or let my heart die. I was forced to put on one of the crimson t-shirts I had refused to wear in the past. Then Dad came back. He marched me to a barber shop in town and had my boyish hair with long fringe cut into a girlish style. After that,

I was taken to a photography studio where my identification card picture was taken. In the picture, my eyes are dull and I look like a psychopath.

In the days that followed, I lost my sense of hunger. I could barely eat half a bowl of rice at mealtimes. Every night, I lay sleepless.

I never again had the courage to mention transsexualism to my parents. I let them believe I had been attacked by some devilish spirit, was cured, and was no longer considering a "sex change." Perhaps they were right, I thought. Maybe it was all my illusion and I was in denial. If they were wrong, at least they had awakened me, albeit cruelly, to the chasm between reality and the ideal. Even if I did know myself as a male, what could I do about it? My impatience had caused me to dash ahead, though I had no money and my parents had never been supportive before. What had I expected? Broken-hearted, I went back into hiding.

This episode must have touched Dad too. For the first time in my life, he left his work to spend time with me, offering to teach me to ride a motorcycle. He showed rare patience in his instruction. During one lesson he told me, "Life is not easy," as if he felt some sympathy for my troubles. His attention, which I was not used to, warmed me up some.

While I spent silent days by the window in the small house, Dad busied himself preparing to send me to college. He was the one who went to the county seat to complete paperwork. He sent neighbors and relatives invitations to the feast in honor of my college admission. He visited the bank on my behalf and booked the tickets for my journey. I should have been grateful, but my depression prevented me from appreciating everything he did for me.

In another shocking turn of events, my parents decided to buy me new clothes to attend university. It was true my clothes were often ill-fitting, ragged and ridiculous. A common outfit might consist of an old orange plaid shirt that had belonged to my niece and was too small for me; a navy blue jacket that had been Dad's, and which I had worn since middle school, even though it hung on me like a sheet; patched and faded jeans passed down from Lan that were so slim my legs looked like chopsticks; and cheap black soccer shoes I purchased for myself. I was accustomed to dressing this way, but my parents held it was improper for university. So, for the first and only time we shopped together as a family, I was taken to the county seat for new clothes.

Stepping into a store intimidated me. My deeply rooted sense of poverty and my body caused me feelings of inferiority, so I felt pressured in the presence of sales clerks. Outside one store, I stopped at a stall displaying jeans and touched the pants.

"Hey, what do you want?" demanded a woman approaching me from inside the shop. When she got closer, her hostile attitude changed. Her voice and face softened. "Sorry, I thought you were a boy," she said.

Like a thief nearly caught in the act, I hurried off.

My parents recommended a girly wardrobe, but my eyes lingered on the clothes for boys. I often bought clothes without trying them on, based on my idealized image of my body. They always turned out to be either too long or too large, since I had ignored my actual body when making my choices. I didn't like trying on clothes. I didn't like shopping at all. That day, I mostly watched, afar and aloof, as we passed stall after stall, visited shop after shop. My parents grew tired and impatient, compromised and urged me to hurry. At last, I selected a light blue shirt and a fitted denim jacket so we could return home.

According to local custom, on big occasions—weddings, birthdays of the elderly, or being admitted to a top university—relatives, neighbors, and friends are invited to a feast, and they are supposed to bring an envelope of money as a gift. The 10,000 yuan for my tuition was collected this way and I was sent to university.

CHAPTER 7

Boy in the Girls' Dorm

In August 2004, Dad and I got on the train to travel to the city where I would attend university. I spent most of the trip watching fields, woods, and roads flash by my window as the train dashed forward. Unaccustomed to new clothes, I sat passively, letting myself be carried into the next stage of life, without aspirations, expectations or visions.

Dad passed me food brought from home: boiled eggs, bread, or tomatoes. He was aging. His hair was turning gray and his every move gave him away as a country man.

From a middle aged couple in the seats opposite us, I perceived a contemptuous glance. The man, in reading glasses with eyes on me, whispered to his wife, "See? Is that a boy or a girl?"

"A boy," the wife replied.

"I say that's a girl," the man said. They argued about it.

I suspected my trimmed hair gave me away. When I rose and headed toward the toilets, their eyes followed me like a tail.

I did not know this was just the beginning of enduring the knives of eyes, but it dawned on me that finally leaving home might not solve my problems. The unknown in front of me might not be any better than the familiar behind me. Sure enough, being gender-assigned female came with extra embarrassment at university.

"You are a girl? You are a girl?" The lady at reception reviewed my papers and then stared at me in amazement.

"Yes," I said, wishing I could answer differently.

I went through all the required procedures and followed all the directions. To our relief, Dad and I learned the tuition would only be 5,000 yuan a year after all. Only art students were charged 10,000 yuan. Although I would be studying at the art school, I was not an art student. The manual sent with my acceptance letter had been unclear.

Our business complete, Dad finally succeeded in sending me and my baggage to the dorm where I had been assigned. I was to live in a narrow room with four bunk beds for eight girls. A row of eight small closets hung from the ceiling on one wall. If a girl wanted to access her closet, she would have to climb onto an upper bunk to reach it. Next to the door was a set of shelves for shared use.

Some of the girls had arrived earlier and already had their beds made. Their parents were helping them settle in. At first, my boy-like appearance set me apart, but we soon got used to each other and the atmosphere became friendly and comfortable. Outside that room, college life was often somewhat complicated for a boy classified as a girl.

"Hey! Boy! Stop! This is a girls' dorm, you are not supposed to enter!"

It was the dorm supervisor posted near the entrance. If the guard did not stop me, it was because she had seen me so often she remembered me. Even so, it seemed she forgot sometimes or there might be a different aunt, who didn't know me, at the post.

Turning back, I would explain, "I live here."

The aunt would scan me up and down, question me and finally let me pass, but her face would still look suspicious. I'd lower my head and go on my way, wishing I could be invisible, but, like anything that does not blend in, I was the center of much attention wherever I went.

Walking up the stairs with all eyes upon me kept me on edge. The staircase was narrow, making it inevitable that girls would brush against me. Then they would whisper to each other. I felt like a beast that was being crowded: hostile and furious. I wanted to seize each one by the collar, shake them and roar, "Damn! Stop looking at me like that! I am not a monster!" Particularly after I first arrived, there was one indignity after another.

In China, military training is compulsory for university freshmen. One day we all gathered in a big hall to receive our uniforms. I was standing in one of the girls' lines when I received the terrible news: there were two uniforms, one for girls and one for boys. The boys would wear navy, the girls would wear red.

I was used to wearing uniforms, but boys and girls wore the same thing in my previous schools. I could bear to wear girly clothes for a few hours or for a day, but I was definitely not ready to wear a uniform that designated me as a girl for a couple of weeks. There was no way around it, however, so I lined up with the girls to receive my costume.

As I moved slowly through the queue, my heart screwed down into a deeply blue mood. Around me, classmates were so excited that they changed into their uniforms right away. Enviously, I stared at the boys while each step took me closer to the front of the girls' line. Finally, a brand new red uniform was placed in my hands. Dejected, I walked through the crowd and left the hall.

Outside, the September sun was shining fiercely in the west. I felt like running, but my legs were too heavy. Anyway, where could I run to? People were everywhere, and where there were people there was the issue of gender. I could not live without people; man was not made to live alone. I wandered with no destination and ended up in a deserted place where I could finally vent my feelings privately. With all my anger, sadness and hatred, I jerked the uniform out of the plastic bag, tore at it, and flung it madly to the withered weeds that sprung from the flagstones at my feet. Shaking, I squatted down, staring at the red uniform. I do not know how long I protested there in silence, but at last I stood up and wiped my tears. I picked up the clothes, slowly packed them into my bag, and headed to the girls' dorm.

There were so many moments like this in my life: moments full of despair because I had no way to resist the cultural forces that surrounded me, no way to live as my authentic self rather than the gender I had been assigned at birth.

If I had been willing to dress like a girl, I might not have been so conspicuous and there would have been less trouble, but who would dress against his nature or will? So, I usually moved about campus during the hours that were less busy, avoiding lunch or dinner time, especially. Once I was in the dorm, I tried not to go out. Once I went out, I tried not to return. Sometimes I lingered outside the building, watching the windows of my room, wishing that I had wings. I could only loiter so long, though, before I had to summon my courage and join the girls filing in and out.

When I got to the sixth floor, where I lived, the climate was different. I was known there and the girls were relaxed around me. At times, they were a little too relaxed for my comfort. On hot days, some of the open-minded girls became nudists. They were natural and poised in their nakedness, perhaps because we were all Art School students and they often drew nude bodies. They walked the corridors without concern that anyone else might feel embarrassed. In the public washrooms, they greeted me with jokes like, "Handsome boy!" While they used basins to pour water over their bodies, I tried to look away, for I felt guilty.

Fortunately, each floor of every teaching building had modern toilet facilities. Since the campus was large, there were frequent times when few people were using the toilets. Before entering, I cased the joint like a thief. When it looked like the bathroom was empty, I slipped into the ladies'. The worst I usually had to deal with was startling some girl when I emerged. Eventually, I realized I could go to the men's room without attracting any attention or being discovered. Since then, I have never entered the women's public toilet again.

The public baths were a serious issue, however. In my hometown, where the weather was cool and dry most of the year, the number of baths people took depended on the season, since homes did not have indoor bathing facilities. In the summertime, some people bathed frequently in the river. At other times of the year, people who cared about personal cleanliness went to a public bath. Almost everyone visited the public baths at the coming of the New Year. It was a tradition to welcome the New Year in this way, and a big project. It could take an hour or two to wash the dust of an entire year off, because by then it had become like a layer of paint that coated the entire body. When one was finished, body and heart both felt lighter.

Since puberty, I had seldom bathed in the river and only bathed properly one or two times a year. Instead of going to the public baths, I washed my arms and legs from a basin, in privacy. As for my breasts, they were shameful evidence of my problems that I did not want to see or touch. My make-shift bathing techniques worked well enough at home, but they weren't going to work at university.

There were no shower rooms in the dormitories, so the public baths were among the most popular places on campus. It was common to see boys or girls in groups of two or three carrying baskets of washing supplies on the way to the public facilities. A common complaint in the dorm was, "Oh my, it has been so long since I bathed; I am so dirty!" During our days of military training, students went to the public baths every other day.

My only private space was my bed, so it was impossible to hide that I never went to bathe. I knew I must appear weird to my dorm mates. I did need a bath, terribly, but how could I enter the girls' shower room without attracting attention? After lengthy consideration, I came up with an idea. I would wear the red uniform as a disguise.

My military training uniform was like a signal, telling people from a distance that the person wearing it was a girl. Indeed, when I wore it, nobody even took a glance at me. It was like armor that shielded me from eyes. In it, I learned how carefree it was to be able to settle into a gender.

The shower room was a wide open space without any curtains or partitions—just shower heads lined up along the walls. Naked female bodies made curved lines floating in the foggy mist. Greetings between acquaintances mixed with the sound of spraying water. Mostly, each young woman concentrated on her own body, scrubbing every corner attentively. Some helped a friend by washing her back. Though nobody took notice of me, I felt uneasy while naked and tried to avoid the sight of my body, especially the breasts that so distressed me.

I glanced at the girl who stood next to me. Her eyes were closed. The water ran along her face and long, dark hair. She was beautiful, like an amorous woman who missed her lover. She looked so content with her body, so content with being a woman. I would have given anything to be so at ease with my own body.

A girl from my dormitory walked up. Her eyes were wide open as if seeing me for the first time. "Brother Jing, you are so skinny!" she said, calling me by the nickname my dorm mates had given me. "Could you do me a favor and scrub my back?" How could I refuse without giving myself away? If our souls had a color, there would have been one in that steamy room that was distinct, but it was disguised by the same female skin worn by everyone around me. So, I played the role expected of me.

I managed to bathe two times in this way before I abandoned my red armor and refused to go back to the women's shower rooms. I decided I would rather stay dirty.

That year, there was a sports tournament at my university. I was honored to be chosen as a member of the parade formation representing our Art and Design department. Remembering the episode in Grade 4, my first concern was what we would be required to wear. As I expected, the uniform for girls was a skirt! There was no way I was accepting that again. I talked to the guy in charge immediately. He was president of the student union of our department, a tall, handsome and fashionable young man. We had just fallen out from afternoon military training and he had come to select the formation members. I presented myself before him wearing my red uniform, which designated me female.

"Excuse me," I said, "could you have me replaced?"

"Why?" he asked. Clearly, my request was unexpected.

"I don't wear skirts," I explained.

He looked at me carefully through his black-framed glasses and excused me from the parade formation.

The girls from the Art & Design department had the best skirts in the parade that year. It was truly a lovely, fresh garment that reflected a spirit of vitality and youthfulness. Only tall girls were awarded the opportunity to wear that skirt and march in the formation. Most of the girls could only admire it. I admired it, too. It reminded me of blooming flowers. As for the girls, I appreciated them and enjoyed seeing them, but I could not admire them.

It was the boys marching in white shirts, black pants and a tie who I admired, or rather, envied. I was jealous of their well-proportioned male bodies, long legs and narrow hips, strong waists and flat chests, wide shoulders and angular faces.

In the city where I attended university, I finally found testosterone. It was available at a drugstore, quite cheaply—just three and a half yuan for a little bottle of white pills. I took several bottles, but the menses did not cease. My voice became lower, which I was happy about, but the side effects were terrible. I have never put on so much weight, before or after, as I did when I was taking that low-grade testosterone. The color of my face turned as ugly as dirt because of the great harm the drug was doing to my liver. Realizing my health was at risk, I stopped taking those cheap pills after about six months. My weight gradually returned to normal and my face appeared healthier after a while, but it had darkened permanently, and my voice remained low.

One day I picked up the phone in my dorm, and the caller on the other end of the line was startled.

"Isn't this the girls' dorm?" someone asked.

Other times, upon hearing my voice, callers would just hang up thinking they had dialed the wrong number. I decided it was better for me not to touch the phone, even though that led to complaints that nobody answered the phone when, actually, I was there. Whatever the difficulties, I was glad my voice changed. My new voice was in accordance with my inner being.

There was, perhaps, one person that year that saw me as more than a girl. Beibei was my classmate and lived in another dorm close to mine. A little stout and short in form, a little dark in color, she was not the prettiest girl on campus, but she had sunshine in her heart, was warm and affectionate, and loved life.

Chinese girls develop intimate friendships easily, however, the relationship between Beibei and I seemed to go farther than usual. She said, without reservation, she was attracted to me. She sat next to me in class, walked with me after class, shared her food with me, and wrote me letters. She gave me unprecedented care and attention, which I had never received from my family. Who can refuse sincere love and kindness? It felt good to be valued.

Gradually, I grew comfortable enough to open up to her. After the lights were out in the dorm, we sat on stools in the corridor and chatted deep into the night. We passed frequent letters. Encouraged by her devotion, I started to gaze at her. Something erotic, not of pure friendship, glittered in my eyes. Embarrassed, she would block my view with her palm. There were times I even reached out to touch her fine, soft hair. A fantasy of a wife was aroused within me, along with a desire to have her all to myself.

One day, I showed her the letter from Dr. Chen and the magazine pages with the article about transsexualism, making her the first friend I ever came out to. It was also the first time she had ever heard the term "transsexual."

I do not know what she was feeling as she learned the news. Shock? Amazement? Bewilderment? She was silent for a while, but finally said, softly, "Creator fools mortals. My heart aches for you."

She did some research online and used the example of Jin Xing—a trans woman and famous dancer in China—to encourage me to be positive. She told me I was special, that I would do something different. A month of vacation was coming up, and she said she was afraid she would miss me too much while we were apart.

The night before she returned home by train, she invited me to sleep in her bed. It was uncommon for two "girls" to be so close they slept in one bed at university. At least in my class, no other girls ever did this. I remember when I woke up the next morning, my hand was on her waist, and I knew she felt it. Some strange feeling seemed to be flitting within her as we lay like that. There might have been more than simple friendship going on during that very intimate act.

Maybe time cooled Beibei's affection. Maybe I was no longer an intriguing mystery. Maybe she was alarmed by our ambiguous relationship and did not know how to proceed, or maybe she was unable to truly accept me as a man and go any further with me. Whatever the cause, when we returned for the next term of our freshman year, she was emotionally distant. She had gone from hot to cold and was like a different person. I was totally unprepared to face such a great fall and found it hard to reconcile in my mind. I came to realize I had developed expectations of Beibei and become emotionally dependent on her. When she was no longer available to me, I became obsessed with retrieving the thing I was addicted to: her loving attention. My disappointment and anger only made her avoid me more. In turn, her increasing indifference made me more frustrated.

My expectations of Beibei had grown into desire and desire had bloomed into infatuation. For an entire term she was the focus of my mind. When I saw her talking or playing happily with other boys, I seethed with jealousy. In the course of time, I tired of longing and accepted I was dreaming of something impossible. More time passed, I made new friends, and finally let go of my obsessive feelings. Eventually, I was able to be at peace when I saw her.

Once the unhealthy aspects of our relationship were over, Beibei and I became friendly again. This time it was a healthy, durable friendship. Even after she married and became a mother, we still remained good friends, and she continued to show understanding and support for me.

CHAPTER 8

Becoming Christian

There were times during my first year at university when I woke up not knowing where I was. I would stare at the ceiling until it occurred to me I was in my bed at the dorms, not on the kang at home. I still felt like where my parents lived was where I was from.

I visited home once a month when I was in high school. Although my parents and I were not close, the short visits reminded me of their existence. University was too far away for frequent visits. I went back only once every six months and we hardly thought of each other the rest of the time.

Once in a while, I would begin to miss my family and wonder how they were doing; however, it took great courage to call home. I would think about it for days, knowing I likely wouldn't receive the comfort I wanted from Mom and Dad. Our calls were often uncomfortable, the conversations ended unhappily, and I was left embittered. My sense of obligation would get the better of me eventually, however, and I would dial their number.

Mom's voice would be harsh. Preoccupied with her work, she'd sound apathetic and perfunctory. She didn't seem to care if I called or not. As for Dad, the call would wake him from his nap on the sofa in front of the television. We would cast around for words and repeat the same topics. Our conversations were rituals; they had nothing to do with emotional connection.

I had always believed my parents should give me my sense of belonging, so I had expectations of our relationship. My time away at university made those assumptions weaker and weaker until they were only a vague sense in the back of my mind. Walking among the crows on campus, I felt like a kite with its string broken, flying along with no direction. My self-consciousness agitated my mind with a flurry of questions: Who am I? Why am I walking here? Where am I going? What am I living for? If the ultimate end is death for everyone, what is all this for? What makes life worth living? Are we just going on out of instinct?

I asked people around me these questions, but no one could give a satisfying answer. They didn't know and they didn't want to be bothered to seek answers. For the confusion with my identity, for the want of love, and for the vanity of life, I needed to find reasons to survive. Otherwise, I would die.

I was terrified to see the face in my mirror. It was sad and wore a bitter look. Because my liver had been harmed from the inferior testosterone pills, my face had become dark and rough as dust. My clothes were old and faded. The form in the mirror was like a shadow of real self. I loathed it. Beibei's rejection convinced me that no one would ever want to get close to me.

One day, I was sitting alone on the terrace facing an open school yard. I felt better away from other people. A foreign, gray-haired man was jogging around the track. White people were rare and enigmatic to most Chinese. I thought, since I had never talked to one before, why not do something new today? Introverted as I was, I acted boldly sometimes. I walked down from the terrace and joined him when he ran past.

Tom became the first foreigner I ever knew. It turned out he was friendly. We had a good conversation while jogging together. When it was time for us to say goodbye, I said, "I heard you foreigners are mostly Christians, and I am also Christian."

Actually, I did not really know what it meant to be a Christian, I had just visited churches, but I was trying to find something we had in common—some way to connect us—because I hoped to see Tom again.

Hearing this, Tom's eyes lit up and he replied, "Really?"

Immediately, I asked, "May I visit you?"

To my surprise, he did not reject this abrupt request from a strange student. So, we made an appointment.

After that, I visited Tom every week and he taught me about the Bible. Tom and his wife, Betty, were not merely teachers, but also missionaries who reached out to students and preached the Gospel. They were regarded and respected by many, including me, as spiritual parents.

Every time we met, Tom greeted me with a firm hug and told me, "God loves you!" or "You are important," "You are precious," "You are a blessing to us." He said these things so seriously that I believed him, though I did not see how I was important, precious or a blessing to them, for I was used to being debased by my family. Over time, Tom and Betty built me up with their words and deeds. I was overwhelmed with gratitude and joy. The world seemed to brighten. What a friend I had found in, not just Tom, but Jesus: the way, the truth, and the life. As promised in Matthew 7:7, I had asked and it was given to me; I had sought and I had found.

Led by Tom, I made the decision to accept Jesus Christ as my savior. My questions were answered, my soul found a home. I read Rick Warren's book, *The Purpose Driven Life*, and came to understand I was created for a purpose and it was only through Him that I could discover that purpose and find out who I am.

At the beginning of my sophomore term, Tom introduced me to a Sister Cui, and entrusted her to take me to the church on campus. Cui was a junior. We happened to be studying the same major in the same department and her classroom was just opposite mine, so I could not hide anything from her. When she asked which dorm I lived in, I told her honestly. Of course she knew that was a girls' dorm. She understood immediately, but kept my secret from Tom.

I came out to Cui and a few other close friends, wanting to be known for who I was on the inside. I hoped they might understand

and stop considering me a girl. Some refused to believe I was a boy, but some were supportive. Cui responded with a long letter:

Dear Lei Jing,

I am so glad you call me sister. I also had a warm and familiar feeling when I first met you. I think it's the Lord who brought us together. I'd really like to take you as my younger brother, to help you in your major, to pray for you every day, to see you grow in the presence of our Father.

Jing, even if you did not talk about it, I can feel the hardships you have experienced, the many times you shed tears to pour your heart out to God, and how many times you are angry with Him because you believe he is truly unfair to you. I can deeply understand the frustrations and inconveniences you have encountered while not being understood, accepted and acknowledged—how you have no sense of belonging. My heart aches for the loneliness, sadness and bitterness you have suffered. I thank God that he gave me a spirit to sense others' pain and see through their eyes. I'm so worried and concerned about you.

Jing, you are the first person I have ever met who has both the temperament of a male and female: resolute and brave, at the same time thoughtful and gentle, you embody the good qualities of boys and girls. Brother, you are very smart; you know God never makes mistakes. Though we feel sorry that God did not create you in the form you prefer, where is the good in regretting? Rather, let's look to the future and think about the plan God has for your life and what His good will is for you, and let's be thankful for all these.

Dear Brother, maybe you don't know yourself what a thoughtful, understanding and warm child you are. In Betty's home, I noticed you disregarding the discomfort of your seat in order to avoid blocking my sight. And you drink so little water; I know you must have your reasons. So many things about you move me and make me admire you, truly. Your experience makes you stand out from your peers and your burdens make you mature. So please, be thankful for everything God has granted you.

Your characteristics of tenderness, gentleness and thoughtfulness, are what boys lack, while your resolute personality and adventurousness is what girls admire or dream of achieving. God gave you what everyone lacks or wishes to have; what everyone else can only be curious about all their lives.

Thus, you appear different in this mundane world, but don't care too much about other peoples' eyes on you. Be thankful to Him first, because he loves you more than anyone.

Brother, having thanked God, perhaps the cloud on your heart will dissipate. Then, I'd like you to read the rest of this letter.

Nowadays, the techniques are so advanced that almost nothing is impossible. As for the doctor you contacted in Beijing, I believe his hospital can do the surgery. But besides trusting modern medical technologies, we should pray to God and seek His help. Prayer should come first, not for our own benefit, but for God's delight. So pray like this:

Oh Lord, thank you for giving me life, no matter male or female. I'm your beloved child, so I give my thanks. Oh Lord, your glory is so abundant upon me that I am distinguished from the majority in this world. Lord, you know everything and you have counted all my bitterness. Oh Lord, if you also grieve for me, make a way for your child! May you make me in the form I wish for and identify with; may you give your child an opportunity to be remodeled. Oh Lord, may you provide everything. No matter the place of operation or the fees, may you supply it yourself. May you also do what you will, give me a miracle beyond what I can imagine. Thank you, my God. In Jesus name I pray, Amen.

I believe He has already listened to you. He will not fail us. He will accomplish everything for you, beyond what your eyes have seen and your ears have heard. God has His own amazing way of doing things. I wait for what we prayed to come true! I hope what we wish is also what God wants!

I wish you happiness every day and a way through your hardships as soon as possible!

Sister Cui

Cui's letter touched me deeply. For the first time, I felt someone had shown great understanding and support concerning my secret burden. Words are inadequate to describe how thankful I felt.

One day, an aunt came to visit Cui. She arranged for us to meet in her dorm, for Cui thought this aunt was spiritual and might give me some counseling and intercession.

When I got to Cui's dorm, the aunt was sitting upright on the edge of the bed. It seemed they were waiting especially for me. Soon Cui and some other friends withdrew from the room, leaving me alone with the aunt. I had not yet gotten used to this strange woman, but I trusted Cui's judgement, so I stayed. Cui's aunt put two mats on the floor before her feet and knelt on one of the mats. She asked me to kneel on the other, facing her. Then she looked me up and down and noticed something.

"What is that on your neck?" she asked. It was a piece of green jade carved in the shape of a tiger. I never knew there was anything improper about it, but she said sternly, "Never wear it again, nor dress like this!"

I felt threatened and was on my guard. Had I done anything wrong? Why was she so bossy and cold, as if the way I was offended her? On what grounds was she giving me commands concerning how I dressed? I concluded my appearance disagreed with her standards and, by trying to correct me, she believed she was helping me. I did not see any virtue in this act, but only the pride of self-righteousness.

During her prayer, the aunt commanded the demon or spirit that caused gender confusion to come out of me. My throat constricted. My heart was ripping. I wished I was brave enough to cover my ears as she denied my natural being in the name of God. The moment she finished praying, I rose and rushed out of the door.

Cui was sorry about this episode, and I learned not every Christian understood transsexualism. They might even consider it sick and sinful. Since then, I have been careful about sharing my secret with any other Christian. At the same time, doubts cropped up in my mind. Was God really displeased with transsexualism? Would he reject me as my parents had? The Lord had become the reason I lived. I hoped he was on my side.

CHAPTER 9

Qingqing

My quest for connection did not end at the door of the church. I was a member of the News Center in the Student Association of Art School. At the beginning of the new school term, we organized a visit to convey our warm regards to the freshmen who were undergoing military training. I was in the group of girls, of course. That night, we walked to the north side of campus where the freshmen were located. We explained our mission to the concierge and went to the floor where the freshmen of the Art School lived. We knocked on some of the doors. Many were out shopping or washing, but a few had stayed inside. They were in pajamas, sitting on the edges of their beds bathing their feet, or just resting.

Our leader was outgoing and maintained the conversation. Good thing, because I was so reticent people took no more notice of me than they did the air. Even so, I felt uneasy in the strange girls' dorms. When we filed out of one dorm and headed to another, I said I would just wait for the rest of the group at the stairs.

I was standing by a wall in a corridor when a girl in pajamas passed me on her way to the bathroom. She was surprised to see me.

"Why are you standing here?" she asked.

I recognized her from one of the dorms my group had already visited. She was the girl who had been putting popcorn in her mouth when we arrived. I hadn't realized she had noticed me.

"I am waiting for the others," I said.

She found it funny that I stood so stiffly. In contrast, she was relaxed and happy. We chatted for a while. She told me her name was Zhang Qingqing and asked for my phone number. That night she texted, "You are good. I like you."

After that, her text messages flowed in, one after another. In the morning, she wished me a good day. At mealtimes, she asked if I had eaten, which in Chinese culture is a way to greet someone and show your concern for them. At bedtime, Qingqing texted, "Good night." She also called frequently and visited me in my classroom, bringing snacks, fruit and other treats.

The enthusiasm and interest Qingqing demonstrated in a "same-sex" friend seemed abnormal to me. It was not that I doubted her intentions, but I could not believe anyone could see through me with any clarity. Her explicitness continuously amazed me. For example, seeing I like children, she said, "If you don't mind, I can bear one for you."

"God's love is sufficient," I replied, "Even if no one else loves me."

"Nonsense," Qingqing said. "Am I not loving you?"

This was extraordinary. In my culture, the word "love" is rarely spoken between friends. It is usually a term reserved exclusively for lovers, and Chinese people often feel embarrassed to say it.

Maybe everybody has something special within, no matter how common she or he appears on the surface. Qingqing had a plain face, but she loved me before she figured out what I was. Regardless of my gender, Qingqing just loved. Her mind was free from the constraints of convention and social principles, which made her different. She had followed her instinct and genuinely took me for a boy, though she had no concept of transsexuality. She didn't question the normality of her affection or care about defining my gender.

On the day of National Holiday in October 2005, I was alone

in my classroom when the door swung open and Qingqing came in. She sat behind me, resting her head on my back, and started to pour out how much she missed me. She confessed she could not fall asleep at night and that she often dreamed about me. She said she worried when she didn't hear from me. In tears, she told me how her heart ached for me. Before I knew it, she was hysterical. The shock I felt left me totally numb. I dared not move or say anything. I could feel her tears, wet and hot, soaking through my shirt.

What had I done to make her feel this way? Her affection was baffling, but I did not refuse it. I felt powerless to say no, though I knew I did not feel the same toward her. She was not my type, either in personality or appearance, but I dealt with the situation by not dealing with it. I just waited to see the outcome. It seemed like such a rare chance to be needed and wanted. How many girls would see beyond the obstacle of my gender issues and truly love me as a boy? Was this not what I had desired all along? If I refused, would there ever be another girl who would feel as Qingqing did?

Since I did not say yes or no, she took my silence as consent. Having made her heart known to me and crossed the boundaries of friendship, Qingqing was delighted and relieved. She stopped crying. Finally, I rose up and she moved closer, holding me tightly as if she was trying to press me into her body. The warmth of her body passed to my nerves. Her lower parts pushed against me with such force something erotic flashed in my head and I thought, "If only I had a penis!" I was embarrassed and felt smothered by such an intimate act, but I did not push her away. We had been strangers just two weeks before. I found it hard to adjust to such rapid change in our relationship.

It seemed an invisible wall had collapsed inside Qingqing, and she was hoping a corresponding wall would collapse within me so there would be nothing between us—the flow of our two souls would merge as one. I hoped no such thing. My heart was shut tightly against this girl who was unattractive to me. But her psychological defenses were down, which allowed me to intrude into her emotional territory.

Without reserve, Qingqing looked up at me, raised her hand, and fondled my hair. A little disgusted, I twisted my head to the side.

"What's the matter? Don't you like me to touch you?" she asked.

Again, I did not answer her. If I told the truth, I might lose my chance to enjoy being wanted and needed as a boy. Though I had little feeling for Qingqing, herself, I was obsessed with being wanted and possessing.

"Laogong," I heard her call me, which means literally: husband. I could not help but shudder at this endearment, used only between couples, but still did not come clean. It's worth mentioning she never called me by my name. Maybe she understood it was not a suitable name for me.

Qingqing told me she had been testing me to be sure I was not a girl. That's when I recalled Qingqing had once asked to go with me to the baths. Seeing I was displeased with the idea, she had begged my pardon. I asked Qingqing if that had been her testing me and she confirmed it was.

We sat for a while until her phone rang. I sent her to the corridor. It was empty and quiet due to the holiday. She turned, tipped toward me, and kissed my cheek, softly and swiftly, before I realized what was happening. Immediately, she left. I was standing frozen, unable to believe what had just happened.

Qingqing's passion for me was fierce and wild. It could not be explained through reasoning. All this because she caught sight of me standing by a wall? How does love start? Is a particular scene enough to cause one to be struck by love? I once asked her why she treated me the way she did. She said she must owe me something from a past life so she had come to pay back the debt. The Chinese, influenced by Buddhism, often speak of past lives.

I was once moved when Qingqing told me she had donated blood in order to get a donor card because she thought it might be useful if I ever had surgery. Nothing she did, however, moved me enough to develop love for her. She never succeeded at touching my heart.

Except to say, "I miss you," "I love you," or to ask me frankly to lie with her, Qingqing had nothing to talk about. Sometimes I grew tired of her repetitive messages and did not reply, which caused her worry. On days when we had drawing class in the mountains, where there was no cell signal, she wouldn't be able to reach me for hours and would suspect I wanted to break up. When I returned to school, she would confront me with her suspicions and cry piteously on the phone. I never explicitly accepted or rejected her, but neither did I try to save our relationship. After a time, we went our separate ways.

The vacancy she left in my life gave me space to reflect. I thought of the times we spent together, and how she had grabbed my hand and laid it right on her chest. I missed that physical intimacy. At least I had been free to touch her if I liked. Poor Qingqing, she was blind to my hypocrisy, greed and selfishness. When I texted, "Will you give me one more chance, honey?" she gladly agreed, perhaps with a little surprise. She obviously hadn't forgotten me.

One winter night in late December, I went to visit her. Under a road lamp, she gazed at me with a fire blazing in her eyes that killed the cold wind. She took the muffler off her face and asked for a kiss. We had our first kiss and I was her first love. We were too young to know what love was, really. We were only carried away by desire, our consciences and purity smeared.

Our relationship lasted about one year. Most of the time, she was a hot coal, while I was cold ice. My indifference and selfishness hurt her. When she could bear it no longer, she finally left me.

CHAPTER 10

Outed

One day, during the second term of my sophomore year, I received a telephone call from Betty, Tom's wife. This was unexpected. Tom was the one who usually called. We arranged to meet at their house and I went as appointed, but when I arrived, Tom did not greet me with a hug. I sensed something had happened.

Tom invited me to take a seat on the sofa and he sat down nearby. He apologized, saying he, as a male teacher, should not have hugged a female student. It was the most absurd apology I had ever heard. It was laughable, yet very sad, to hear him ask forgiveness for showing me the affection I so desperately needed. I realized someone must have gabbed. Who was it? I didn't really want to dig into it, lest I resent the telltale. Perhaps the person who outed me thought they were performing a kindness. If so, it was an unwanted kindness to me. I could just imagine the dialogue: "You should know Lei Jing is a girl!"

When I first met Tom and Betty, I had not corrected them when they referred to me as "he," because I didn't—and don't—think there was anything wrong with it. I had not meant to deceive them purposely and didn't even take notice of the pronoun they used when referring to me. But after Tom's apology, they began to use the pronoun "she." It was galling and I yearned to say, "Please don't." But on what grounds could I protest? Was I not living in the girls' dorm? Did my identification card not say "female"? Did my body not have female parts? What had I expected to be called? There were times I wanted to rush out of that house, but I had found love and warmth there. How could I break with them? Who can resist love?

After apologizing, Tom kept properly aloof and Betty took over with me. I shared with Betty that I longed for surgeries. Her reply was desperate: "If God was pleased by you having surgeries, I would give you the money. If Jesus appeared at your door, he could have your body changed, but he would not do that."

I will never forget how firmly Betty insisted that God created me a girl and that I was living lies. She wanted to "help retrieve" my gender identity as a girl. In her belief, there was something distorted in my authentic gender identity—or perhaps Satan had stolen my heart—and God's purpose for me was to live as a girl. According to Betty, I was deviating from that purpose.

After hearing her judgement, I did not know what I was anymore. In what way should I come before the Creator? When I came to him as I genuinely was, people told me my existence was wrong, the result of sin, and displeasing to God. Did they expect me to be a hypocrite, presenting myself to God as something I was not?

I broke down, for God was the very breath of my life, the reason I lived. If God did not accept me as I was, I would have to deny the essence of myself or lose my Christian faith. A wall had been built between the Divine and me. That wall was spiritual authority's belief that transsexualism is a sin.

I grieved, knowing that my intrinsic being was considered against the law of God. My innermost being was beyond my ability to change. It was like some program rooted in my brain before I was self-conscious. My mind and actions were directed by it, and I did not function like a girl, but God had not given me a male body. The software and hardware were incompatible. Did that mean He intended me to be a woman or a man?

Betty was anxious to reprogram me. We had long, intimate talks. I described my childhood and how I was treated by my parents. From

Betty, I heard the phrase "verbal abuse" for the first time. She said it had distorted my self-image. "Abuse" is a horrible word. It made me shudder and stirred my hatred and rage. Could it be the cause of my transsexualism?

This concern made me press on. To this day, I do not know how I managed to form the words, but somehow, I disclosed my darkest secret: when I was very young, I had suffered sexual abuse from my brother, Boy, and the teenaged son of my neighbor.

Pieces of those memories always haunted my brain. They were shameful and heavy. Oh, I wished I could wipe them out! Could the memories have been implanted in my head if the events had not truly happened? Was there any way for me to forget those scenes where Boy removed my pants: in the aperture of the bridge, on the kang in his room, inside a hut in a field, over and over in so many places. Must I remember so clearly the neighbor boy calling out to me when I was climbing the fence on my way home? Calling me to come over to his house. . .oh, his lustful eyes! When all that happened, I had been too young to know how to protect myself. The deeper I went into my memory, the more I vowed I would kill them and burn down their houses if I could.

When these memories were roused, hatred for my parents gripped me. Why had they left me home alone when I was so young? Why had they been so careless with me? If I had been tended and protected—if these crimes had not been committed against me— would I have been happier? I had always wondered if being molested had turned me transsexual.

What if Betty was right? She said I was living in falsehood, under the spell of Satan's lies. That the devil had stolen the girl's heart out of me! Was that true? Was everything I believed about myself and pursued for my life just wrong? My heart wrung with anguish at these thoughts.

Seeing my agony, Betty wanted to show me some scriptures. She opened a Bible to Matthew 5:3 and I stammered through:

> "Blessed are the. . .poor in spirit, for theirs is. . .the kingdom of heaven. . .Blessed are those who mourn. . ."

Triggered by the word "mourn," I choked, and then unable to

hold back anymore, wept. All the sadness of the past, all the taunts and indifference I had endured, the anger and struggles, the conflicts with my faith, the disillusionment and hopelessness, swept over me. I did not know who I was anymore, or how I should live.

I wept so hard, I do not know how much time passed. Betty knelt on the floor, holding me in her arms. After a while, she rose and stood behind me. She laid her hands on my shoulders and started to sing. The song was peaceful. It had a calming power. Gradually, I came to my senses. Finally, I was able to rise from the chair and stagger out.

After the episode at Tom's and Betty's house, I felt like I was trapped in a large glass cage. I could see everybody around me moving, talking and laughing, but I was just not able to be one of them. I was sure they were sizing me up as if I was a beast in an exhibit—whispering, head to head, and exchanging opinions, while I had nowhere to hide.

"Let me out!" I was yelling inside, but the glass cage created a vacuum that no sound could exit.

In my mind, competing noises echoed so loudly it seemed they would burst my ears. I beat the walls of my mental cage wildly, trying to escape, but they would not break and were so high I could not see over them. I was scared and disheartened. I dared not look up at a passer-by, or visit a barber shop, or step into a store.

There were students who had committed suicide on campus. Some drowned themselves, some hanged themselves, some jumped out of a building. It seemed I might be next. I imagined many ways to terminate myself. The voice of death whispered to me, "Jump and you will be relieved." I imagined the wind blowing by my ears, the moment my body reached the ground, how everything would then be over in a pool of blood. I envisioned walking step by step into the deep water of the sea, the waves sweeping over me, my body resting eternally on the seabed. Watching train carriages pass by, I saw myself lying on the track, felt how the coldness of the iron would seep into my back, how the airflow would press against me as the train drew closer and closer, how my body would finally be crushed.

Death had become alluring. It had never seemed so real and close before. But, I had always been taught, "Thou shalt not kill, not even yourself. The person who commits suicide is unforgivable and deserves hell." The turmoil of this life might end with suicide, but another kind of torture would arise. Even if that was not so, death couldn't exactly fulfill my deepest wishes.

What I longed for was an end of everything, to turn back time and get rid of my flesh. Like Job, I wanted to have never been born, never been in the world at all. With no way to accomplish that dream, I lived mechanically and passively, like a raft drifting far out at sea. I could see no welcoming island, nor any companion who shared my afflictions, nor did I know where the tide of time would take me. I had given up my initiative for living.

Betty's contract with the university expired at the end of my sophomore year. She left China, so I had no more spiritual oversight. I seldom visited the church. There, they sang joyfully at the end of Sunday services: "The world is more wonderful because of you, no one is like you, oh you are so special in God's eyes, no one can replace you." These lyrics chafed my spirit. I cursed my life and wished someone could replace me. Everyone else in the church was so happy and content, praising God's goodness, while I sank into the mire of self-pity. Also, they called me "sister." I hated that.

I was profoundly envious of one leader of the church, though he was nice to me. He had everything I dreamed of: he could marry if he wanted, have children if he wanted. To him, God was good and life was beautiful. He closed his eyes when he prayed, basking in God's favor. I looked at him, how immersed he was, such a lucky dog. I was aggrieved by thoughts that God was partial to some people, yet he had given me a terrible fate and only looked on with his arms folded.

What was the point of such cruelty? If I was not to be allowed a decent life, why create me at all? Unable to see anything but my misery, I grew bitter and angry with God. So I stopped attending church.

I had a Christian friend during that time, Xiaowen, who tried her best to encourage me. Because she thought I was a girl when we first met, Xiowen had no qualms about getting close to me. When I eventually came out to her, Xiowen did not seem concerned. After that, I don't think she considered me truly a male or a female, but one way or the other, it didn't change our friendship. Between the two of us, we wrote hundreds of text messages sharing our thoughts, feelings and the trifles of life over the next year.

Xiaowen saved our messages and at the end of our junior term, handed me a heart-shaped box. To my surprise, inside was a thick pile of heart-shaped notepaper. She had written down almost every message I had sent her. There was my depression, spelled out:

I don't like myself. How can I like myself? I don't know what to do or what to hope.

I'm not a good child of God. I don't know how to stop the pain.

Nothing makes me happy, I want to kill myself.

I don't feel like going anywhere, my state is bad.

I hope I can die quietly, alone.

Under each of my messages, Xiaowen had written an encouraging reply:

Lei Jing, we can't abandon everything and live alone, because we all need to be loved and heard. Though people who truly listen are rare, we need some kind of circle. . .so keep going to the church, even though you don't want to. It's God we go to meet, not people.

You are anguished, but God gave you gifts that nobody else has. You are such a special child, I don't know why you have been given so much pain and I don't know God's plan for you, but I know he will do his work himself in his own time. His time won't be wrong. Find a way to get close to God and cast all your pain onto Him. God will save you from the pain.

Lei Jing, we both know there are miracles with God, but we believe miracles can only happen to others while we, ourselves, have nothing to do with miracles. Let's believe miracles will happen to us too, just once, ok?

And finally,

As I wrote down your messages, I found your agony did not ease as time went by, so I don't think time is the best cure. When I think of you, I feel quiet and sad. Suddenly, I have nothing to say because words are impotent.

She was right. Time was not curing my depression. I felt no one understood me, and I could not expect to be understood. I realized what people said about me was only their beliefs, but I also had a deep need to be loved and accepted as my authentic self.

For about a year, I avoided church and contact with other Christians. I thought staying away from God, his church and his people, would give me some relief from my internal conflict. At least I would not be reminded of it again and again. If the pain of it was less acute, perhaps I could survive that way—blindly, with my senses shut off—until the natural termination of my life finally relieved me for good.

CHAPTER 11

Shao Han

During the 2007 summer vacation, a Bible study group was being held by a Mr. Lee. He was a Korean missionary who reached out to the students and was respected by them. A sister from the church named Shao Han invited me to join Mr. Lee's group. She said Mr. Lee's Bible study was a smaller group that would not make me uneasy. So I joined them during the days before I left for home.

At the close of one session, Mr. Lee asked if we had any questions. I did, but even thinking of it unnerved me. Several times the words rose to the edge of my mouth, but I swallowed them back down. Would he be like Betty? Give an answer that would peel back my scars and make me face what I was trying to escape? Perhaps it was better to keep my own counsel and get out of there as soon as the meeting was over.

Mr. Lee, however, was in no hurry to end the Bible study. There was a short period of silence, as if to give me an opportunity, and the question was trembling inside my mouth, on the verge of rushing out. Finally, I summoned enough courage and asked, "Can one have his gender changed?" More precisely, I wanted to know if one could make his body conform to his soul.

On hearing this, a girl sitting with Shao Han was shocked, her eyes wide open. Was she wondering how I came up with such a question and astonished to realize this boyish "girl" sitting across from her was actually thinking of a "sex change"? Han was smiling, as though glad to learn something new about me. I turned my eyes to Mr. Lee and waited nervously for his answer. To him, it was a plain question, and he did not seem to think it was strange that I raised it.

Gently and slowly, in his not-so-fluent Mandarin, he said, "One can change his gender." I think what he really meant was a person could change the physical properties of the body, not the innate sense of gender. His manner and voice indicated he did not have a problem with people being transgender.

Receiving this totally different answer from another respectable and popular spiritual teacher, I did not know whom to believe, but I came to know different people held different opinions on this matter.

After Han heard my question in Mr. Lee's Bible study, she seemed to have a subtle change of attitude toward me. Gradually, our text messages and calls became more frequent. From time to time she came to visit me in my dorm and shared the message she had heard during Sunday services, in her own words, to convey the spirit of that week's church meeting. Once we sat on low stools on the balcony, and she explained the signs of being saved to me, point by point, according to the notes she had taken. She leaned forward to show me the scripture in her Bible and her breasts, like twin fawns, peeped out of her low-necked shirt. My eyes were trapped in that enchanting cleavage and not interested in being liberated, but I knew it was not right to gaze at others' privates on purpose and I forced them away. My mind was not so easily freed. It was in a flurry lingering on that image. All this happened in a flash. Shao Han noticed nothing and went on speaking with pleasure, but I doubt I caught everything she said.

Han was a joyful, sanguine girl. She smelled like sunshine and was bright and healthy, outwardly and inwardly. She had a mild disposition that was like a polished stone: comfortable to rub up against. She dressed comfortably too, often wearing sneakers, a backpack, and her hair tied in a ponytail, which made her appear nimble. Behind her glasses fluttered thick eyelashes. The color of her lips and teeth showed her good health. Her face was fair and lean, which suited her graceful neck.

We often sat on the edge of a road chatting in the light of the streetlamps. She liked to banter and seemed totally immune to my gloom and silence. She talked with self-mockery and a sense of humor; the words she used were colorful and the way she described things was amusing. She often had fun by imitating my expressions and the way I said, "ah," "hm," and "aye." Her mimicry never failed to cause her to burst into laughter and I laughed with her. At times like that, it was as if I had become another person, a person who could joke freely and give a hearty laugh.

One day, Han and I were the only people in the dorm. She had been very casual with me. She climbed onto my bunk and lay there, while I sat on a chair. There was a hush in the autumn air. I vaguely knew she understood me and did not simply consider me a girl. She had never called me by my girly name, just as Qingqing never did. I had taken Han as my good friend, and I always hoped the friends I valued would know me according to my heart, rather than my body. I broke the silence and said, "I will have surgeries," though I did not know how, when or where at that moment.

Han remained still on my bed. I could not see her expression. She did not try to persuade me to change my mind, nor show she was astonished. "No matter what you are like or will do in the future, I will stand by you," she said.

I was not surprised at her response, somehow, but I was relieved, knowing that she accepted me. In front of Han, I did not need to conceal myself. The person huddled inside me seemed to stretch out, so she got to see a different me that others never saw.

I liked Han, expected her to come to me, and enjoyed her presence. Sometimes, I felt an impulse to spread my arm around her waist or watched her lips when she spoke and imagined pressing a kiss on them. She saw us a little differently, though, saying with a smile, "You are a very good person. Let's be neighbors in the future. I will live upstairs, you downstairs, so I can entrust you with caring for my children."

I was afraid I would become too emotionally dependent on her, too fascinated by her if we got closer. I had learned my lesson from the relationship with Beibei. When she had distanced herself from me, texting and calling less, I had felt sad and regretted my expectations of her. I had written in my diary, "Some girls are attracted by my male temperament. Because of my social identity as a girl, they can approach me without scruple and have their curiosities satisfied, but they do not want me, no matter how much they like me." I believed Shao Han felt the same way.

When Han seemed distant, I did not grasp for her. When she came back to me, I did not refuse her. I took things as they came, not knowing how our relationship would end. Maybe it would resolve itself after we were parted by graduation.

Usually, when the weather turned cold, the leaves withered and fell, and it began to drizzle, which made me at a loss over what to do with the desolation inside me. But that October was different. It was as if a stove was lit within me that burned away loneliness and depression, because Shao Han was with me. During the days of National Holiday, we were together almost every day.

At that time, we were relocated to a new campus that was under construction. Surrounding the compound of buildings was undeveloped land, farms and woods. Shao Han and I often strolled in those rarely traveled places and had great fun exploring nature. Days were clear as water; our minds were at ease and free. One night, we were strolling along a bumpy path. The outline of vegetation was only dimly visible in the dark. Han put her hand in one of my sleeves for warmth. Her loose hair was flying over her face, and we laughed like two drunkards. Then we looked up to the stars and suddenly a golden line flashed across the night sky.

"Did you see it?" Han asked, pointing with her other hand. We gazed, lost in the moment, trying to track where the meteor had gone. I wondered if all beautiful things would pass in a twinkling like that meteor. What lasts for long?

Another day of that holiday, we went to visit the market that sold decorative materials. We were hunting for suitable items for one of my assignments. We got off the bus and started to cross the street. Han took my arm. I always felt insecure in public. It was as if the very air was full of thorns prickling my skin. I was shy about stepping into shops, worried people would ask, "Are you a boy or a girl?" But arm-in-arm with Han, I felt secure. She seemed to know my weaknesses and to want to help me get through them. I could feel her sincerity, for which I was thankful.

The market was like a big maze with rows of shops selling every imaginable thing: kitchen and bath products, tiles, lamps, paint, decorations, everything associated with the home. It kindled my imagination. Would I have a home one day? A home furnished with these articles? A home where my wife and children lived? Or was all that impossible?

We bought nothing, but feasted our eyes. By the time we left the market, it had started to rain. Neither of us felt like going back to campus. Han suggested we ride the bus, but where should we go?

I suggested we go to Shanhaiguan, the location of the first pass of the Great Wall. Han agreed, so we got on a bus and enjoyed the view of buildings, pedestrians and vehicles outside the window.

At Shanhaiguan Pass, we held hands and walked along the pavement. No one else was there. Apparently, people had gone indoors to hibernate away from the damp, cold weather. The shops of traditional architecture on both sides of the road were closed. They looked like they had fallen asleep in the drizzle.

All the worries of reality dropped away. It was the first time Han and I had held hands that way. When our hands separated, they were drawn back together, as if they harbored magnets. Both of us felt the subtle change in the air between us and the change was in our hearts, as well. Despite the dreary autumn weather, the warmth between us felt like sunbathing in a spring breeze, though we did not speak of it.

We turned into a side lane and discovered ourselves in a village. We explored its maze of lanes: stepping over puddles, passing by old wooden doors, taking note of the marks time had left on the stone carvings, and how fresh the withering flowers looked bathed in raindrops. A moment came when I realized we were like lovers traveling in some faraway place. Temporarily distanced from the circle of dorm and class life, we were able to be more authentic with each other. I liked the person I was able to be when I was with Han.

On the way back, our minds awakened to reality. Sitting in the bus, holding my hand, Shao Han asked me, "Am I the first one? Will I also be the last one?" It sounded like she was asking us both, not really expecting an answer from me, just uncertain of herself.

I watched her, feeling a spasm of heartache. I did not know how to reply. Who was I, after all? Only a balloon floating in the sky at the mercy of the wind without direction or backing. I could not give any promise; I saw no option for the happiness of marriage.

Back at campus, it was time for us to separate. We stood face to face on the edge of a desolate land with no words for our ambiguous relationship. Should we proceed recklessly or leave things as they were? We did not know what measures to take; the results were unpredictable. With an umbrella in one hand, Han spread her arms around me as if to say, "I am sorry I can't be with you, but I hate to part from you." I held her too, giving her silent thanks for her company.

There was an orchard near the campus, just down an earthen slope, and there was a poplar wood by a broken wall of red bricks. This was my favorite place to wander. One day, another figure joined me in the woods. The afternoon sun shone through the branches rendering the sparse yellowish leaves radiant. Shao Han and I walked below the trees, immersed in ourselves. At one end of the wood was a large stone. I sat down on it. Han sat on my shoes and leaned against my lower legs. She said she was tired and closed her eyes, sinking into some meditation. Occasionally, she asked if my legs were growing numb. Her soft hair was right before my eyes and I was tempted to touch it, but I dared not move lest she be disturbed. I liked having her so close to me. We sat in this silence and became a statue, forgetting time, until the sun set and the moon rose, till night fell and lights were lit.

We finally rose to go back to campus, but Han would not leave. She held me tightly for a long time, postponing the hour we must part. A song I had heard and liked floated through my mind:

When the breeze kisses the treetops,

The night is just right,

For you're still here by my side.

Look at the lights,

Why feel sad, why sigh?

Tonight will never be found again,

Come and embrace with me while there is time.

Stay by my side,

Don't wake me up,

Oh, sweet night.

We stood so close I could feel the warmth of Han's face. She quivered and gasped, afraid, yet expecting. Our noses touched. Then our lips.

When we had to depart, realizing her affection had betrayed her reason, Han cried, "Don't make me fall in love with you! I'll get married. I'll have children."

I stood transfixed, watching her, but not knowing what to say. I had never believed we would cross the boundary of friendship and become lovers through a kiss.

Despite Han's struggles, the joy of falling in love overcame her misgivings. Being in love is like taking a pain killer. A new lover is like a shining sun that disguises every cloud.

My dream of love was finally fulfilled and a person I liked felt the same way. In front of Han, I lived out myself. I was loving and loved as my real self.

I learned love is like a drug that is so addicting lovers miss each other every moment. A day apart seems like three seasons. Rather than easing desire, new love stirs up its flames and makes people thirst for more. Under love's spell, illusions are taken for truths, temporary passions believed eternal. But nobody warned us. Who could have told us anyway? Even if we had been advised, even if we believed the advice, would we have been able to discipline our emotions or behaviors? I doubt it.

That winter, Han prepared for postgraduate entrance exams and we often met at night on the grounds near the library where she studied. Sometimes, thinking of the impossibilities, I felt like giving up. It was impossible to get married, impossible to have children, impossible to last long. What were we doing?

Han worried and doubted at first, but she soon became optimistic. "To me, you are no different from other boys," she said. "You know I care about you. You know I am the woman who will become your wife. When you said you hurt, I ached with you. Smile. How charming you are when you smile. I can recognize you from among millions of people if you smile. Everything will be fine."

Her tone and expression convinced me she was serious and resolute. Eventually, I believed we would last.

Because of her studies, Han seldom went to church that winter. I did not go for the sake of my feelings and other peoples' eyes. Neither of us loved God to such an extent we could overcome these hindrances to worship among his people. God was not as appealing or practical as a touchable lover. So, we both detached from the body of Christ. We were like sheep wandering the hills: free, but without spiritual protection.

Having a girlfriend increased my longing for a masculine body. I was more motivated than ever. Getting surgery, especially top surgery, felt more pressing. I wished I had been born tall and strong so I could shield Han from the cold wind. I wished I had broad shoulders for her to lean on.

CHAPTER 12

Hormones and Hospitals

At the end of 2007, I learned about another brand of testosterone while browsing an Internet chat room for transsexuals. The testosterone was a prescription drug, but I was able to get access to it through certain online channels. It was a luxury to have it. Even back then it cost 45 yuan per pack and the price has been steadily rising. It is over 50 now, and one pack only lasts four days. A month's supply cost me almost one-fourth of my salary. It has very few side effects, though. Perhaps that is why it is so expensive. Its effect on my body wasn't so obvious either. Maybe that was because I did not take enough, according to the instructions. I used a reduced dose so I wouldn't run out of it too quickly, and there were times I couldn't afford to buy it at all. Psychologically, it comforted me and brought me a sure, secure feeling. Physically, it worked subtly, making my face look more masculine. By the time I graduated university, I was able to easily merge into society as a male, albeit one who looked abnormally young for his age.

I longed for top surgery day and night. Four years earlier, Dr. Chen Huanran had written that we could talk about my condition after I graduated university. In 2008, I visited the hospital he had written from, but was told Dr. Chen had resigned. It was a setback, but I refused to give up.

There is another famous doctor, He Qinglian, who is respected as the father of transsexuals in China. In the late 1980s, he performed the first gender confirmation surgery reported in China. Chinese transsexuals call him Father He.

I wrote to Father He at the beginning of 2008. It was said he replied to everyone who wrote to him, and he sent me a brief letter saying he understood and giving me his phone number and office hours. So I went to Shanghai to visit the hospital where he practiced: 411 Hospital of Chinese People's Liberation Army. This is the hospital where most gender confirming surgeries are performed in China. I missed seeing him. Dr. He was not on duty that day, but Dr. Zhao, who was considered Father He's successor, received me. Dr. Zhao called me "young man," and I believed he understood transsexuality very well. As it turned out, Dr. Zhao was doing most of the operations by that time because Father He was retiring.

It was in Dr. Zhao's office that I met a trans woman for the first time. She is the only trans woman I have met so far. She came in to have her throat checked. It had just been operated on and there was a gauze cover over it. She was in a patient suit and was tall and slim, with long hair. Her eyes looked a little sad and clear; her voice and movements were soft. I could not imagine her as a man. I believed she was a woman, despite her body. I wondered if people would feel the same about me, if they would find they could not associate me with a woman. Dr. Zhao told me, "Her family was severely against her, so she fled from home, but her family came to see her in the hospital afterwards. It is a pity she is unable to produce children."

The surgeon discussed my options with me, but without money and the support of family, I knew I couldn't actually do anything. Maybe I just wanted to feel the pulse of my dream, to smell the air of that hospital and pass by the rooms where many transgender people had lay recovering from their surgeries—like gazing through a shop window where the very thing I was dying to buy was displayed, shining and glorious. I wanted to get closer to it and see it from behind the glass, so I went inside and consulted with the shopkeeper, but unable to buy, I had to leave without it.

From the time I knew I could resort to surgeon's knives, I had been watching the hospitals of every city I occupied. The bus I took home every month during high school stopped at the county hospital. I used to gaze out the window at that building, imagining having my female organs removed there if I could save enough money.

In college, I visited the small hospital at my university to consult about having my ovaries removed to prevent menses. The doctor, a middle-aged woman, looked through her glasses at me, stunned and bewildered.

"But, I can't see that you are a girl. . .you have breasts?"

I unzipped my black coat. The moment her hand touched my shirt on the right side of my chest, she was convinced. She was kind and understanding, but could not help. Even if the hospital was capable of such an operation, they would not do it, nor was I able to pay. Still, I continued to approach hospitals and doctors, every year or two.

At the famous Peking Union Medical College Hospital, I wandered about the big building, though I didn't have an appointment or know who to talk to about my condition. Eventually, I discovered a waiting area full of cold seats. I was lost. I did not know what to do, there was nothing I could do, yet I refused to leave. Vacantly, I watched the patients passing in front of me. The hospital seemed like a large factory that repaired the machinery of human bodies. I wished they could take out my heart and see what was wrong with it. Why had it rejected its own body? Why was it so restless? If a car was broken, it could be sent to its manufacturer, but to whom could I be sent? I was ill, but not physically. I felt like yelling, "I need a doctor!"

Actually, in order to qualify for surgery, I needed a lot more than a doctor. When I first began exploring my options, every plastic surgeon and hospital had their own criteria for accepting patients. In 2009, the Ministry of Health published the first Chinese management standards for gender confirming surgery. This demonstrated the right to get surgery, but the qualifications are strict and difficult. For instance, hospitals were required to have a plastic surgery department for at least 10 years, which means no new treatment centers providing gender confirmation surgery can be established.

According to the new specifications, I would have to prove I have no criminal record and am unmarried. A year of psychiatric treatment must be completed to show I cannot be persuaded to change my mind about surgery. I would also have to notify a parent and obtain his or her consent. If I somehow managed to meet all the conditions for approval, I would still need the equivalent of a few years' salary to pay for the surgeries.

After gender confirmation surgery, I would have the right to change the gender marker on my identification card, but updating my school records would be nearly impossible. There is no law allowing for retroactive change to academic records, so I would be at the mercy of the personal opinions of a long line of academic bureaucrats. I would most likely be forced to resort to forgery or altered photocopies.

Technically, surgical transition was possible. Realistically, there were—and are—a lot of roadblocks. Recent studies estimate there are about 400,000 transgender people in China, but according to the two surgical facilities that do most of the gender confirmation surgery here—Changzheng Hospital and Shanghai Ninth People's Hospital—only 800 people have received operations there over the past 30 years. Some transsexual people travel to other Asian countries for their surgeries, because it is easier and less expensive in places like Thailand, but that was still too expensive for me. Despite all these obstacles, which I could find no way around, I remained obsessed with getting surgery to bring my outer body into harmony with my inner gender.

I once asked a very mature and spiritual sister I respected, "What do you think of people who are transgender."

She knew me as a man and had no idea I was transsexual. She responded, "They are people who do not accept their gender."

I think that is the opinion of the majority, but I know differently. I accept my gender. I know I am a man, regardless of the shape of my visible body. Alas, wherever I go, I must carry this body with me. Whatever I do, I do it through this body. I need it for every motion and every physical experience. Other people fit me into their mental context based on my appearance. My body is the only thing that prevents me from being recognized and accepted as who I am. People understand and show sympathy when a baby is born blind, deaf or without limbs. If baby is born with both male and female genitalia, or no sex organs at all, we have learned we only need to wait until the child is older. The child will know his or her gender. But my authentic identity is disregarded. I had no choice over the discord between my body and soul. Yet, it has caused me so much pain, I have been willing to give everything I have to bring the two together and be true to myself.

CHAPTER 13

Baptism

On a bright day in April 2008, I traveled to Beijing to visit Shao Han. She had failed the exams for graduate school, but found a job and relocated the previous month.

The square of Beijing Station was forever bustling with comers and goers. Crowds of people—rural workers, students, travelers and businessmen from every place in the nation—mingled in that city every day. Transient laborers sat there with their luggage and bound quilt as if waiting for something. Tourists wearing identical clothes and hats followed guides who led their groups with a flag and loudspeaker. Women in *topi* bearing signboards that advertised hotels sought lodgers among the recent arrivals. Beggars and frauds hunted for targets. A super large LED screen above the square broadcast the news, interspersed with station announcements: "XXX train from X City to Beijing is arriving on platform. . ." After that, a new flood of people would flow through the square.

The moment I saw Shao Han, who was waiting for me in the sunlight, the hubbub of voices, the moving figures, the rushing traffic, everything, seemed to recede. Her glasses were off and she was lightly made up with her smooth hair down around her face. She wore a yellow t-shirt and tight jeans. A white handbag hung from her shoulder. The casual college student in sneakers and a back pack was gone, Shao Han was fashionable and her feminine beauty was evident. I smiled while walking toward her, proud she was my girl.

I was only there for a short visit. Graduation was coming up and I still had to finish a project. But I hoped to find work in Beijing so I could stay near Han after college.

I stayed in a room where Han had been living in the basement of a modern residential compound. She had moved to another place several days before, but the rent was paid until the end of the month, so it made sense for me to use the room. That night, the janitor of the building knocked on my door and asked to register my identification.

"Because of the Olympics being held here in August, all people lodged in Beijing must be registered," the janitor explained.

Though I rarely used my identification, I had it with me, just in case. I reluctantly handed it to her.

The janitor looked over my identification and said, "This is fake! It is not yours."

I said it was indeed mine.

"Are you not a man? It says 'female.' How can it be yours?" she asked. "You must leave if you don't have ID."

I was happy she believed I was male, so I did not argue. My plan was to leave the next day, anyway, so it was fine. But this was the first time I encountered this type of issue with my identification. Realizing the difficulties I could expect to face in the future, I was troubled.

The next day, Han and I went sightseeing at the 798 Art District, a famous art community housed in a decommissioned military-industrial factory complex. While we were there, I saw an interesting job notice on the wall of a gallery. As soon as I got back to campus, I emailed my resume, noting on it I was a Christian. I thought it would be great if the person who read my resume happened to be Christian, too. Perhaps my disclosure would make my resume stand out to the interviewer.

Soon, I received a call inviting me to interview. The caller spoke English in a mature male voice and he was impressed I could respond so fluently. He also asked about my spiritual status with questions such as, "How long have you been a Christian?" and "Which is your favorite book of the Bible?"

A few days later, I travelled back to Beijing. When I arrived at the gallery, I got a surprise. Mr. Zhao, the man who had called me, was sitting in a wheel chair and obviously accustomed to it. He handled the chair as if it was an extension of his own body. For his part, Mr. Zhao was surprised to see I looked like a teenager of 15 or 16 and said so. It was almost heartbreaking to hear my appearance and mind were at such odds. Understanding how young I looked to others was a knock to my self-esteem. Mr. Zhao, however, did not change his attitude toward me. He had already started thinking of me as one of his team members and demonstrated great trust in me.

Without reservation, he explained the ideals, goals and plans of the gallery—a subject he was passionate about. Mr. Zhao's brain was highly efficient, his mind was clear and calm, his thoughts were deliberate and organized. He had a sense of urgency about time, which drove the people in his environment. He was serious and conscientious about his work, but he treated his staff with respect and concern. His charm was appreciable immediately.

I was disconcerted about my identity. I wanted to tell him the truth, for sooner or later I would have to present my identification. After we went to his office and were alone, I said faintly, "I have something to tell you before you decide whether or not to hire me. I'm. . .actually transsexual. My ID is female."

Mr. Zhao turned out to be a man who did not judge by outer appearances. He remained calm and did not change his mind about me. I could not believe he accepted me as a brother, despite the facts I had just revealed, but he did what he could to reassure me.

"Ok. I'll keep this secret for you. I won't tell anyone, not even my wife," he said. Mr. Zhao's wife was Art Director for the gallery.

Then I explained I wanted to have surgeries.

"I noticed you referred to 'I' three times in one sentence," Mr. Zhao responded.

His insightful remark was a wake-up call that struck me dumb.

I was ashamed to realize I focused too much on myself, though it would take me a long time to fully understand the impact of being so self-absorbed. I am still learning that lesson, and perhaps will be all my life.

Mr. Zhao shifted the conversation, asking whether or not I had been baptized. I said no. I had rejected baptism in the church because I refused to be called "sister."

"You should be baptized," he said. He felt it was imperative and wanted me to understand the truth about baptism.

That night, in his house, Mr. Zhao taught me from the Bible. He was obviously a scholar. He knew exactly where to find every verse he referred to and he was an apt teacher. For the first time, the verses jumped out and became vivid and all linked together for me. My eyes were opened to how the words were alive and relevant. Because of his explanations and genuine acceptance of me as a brother, I was overwhelmed by gratitude for God and my love for the Lord was kindled once again.

I was baptized into Christ as a brother by Mr. Zhao and then he hugged me affectionately. We both believed our meeting was no accident, but had been arranged by God.

Mr. Zhao inspired me to consider my focus might be wrong. Compared to God and one's spiritual being, the form of the body was not so vital. I paid too much attention to my body. My obsession with changing the form of my body was consuming my energy and spirit. I was missing things that were more important, in particular, strengthening my personal relationship with God, regardless of what people did or said about me. If I got to know He who created me, I might be able to truly know myself. As for my body, it was temporary, something that would pass and could be surpassed. Life could be lived beyond the body, as Mr. Zhao demonstrated. He was paralyzed physically, but faithful to God and a living witness, giving off the fragrance of Christ as Paul describes in Second Corinthians.

Mr. Zhao had earned his MBA from Harvard. For no obvious reason, just in the prime of his life, he suddenly became paralyzed. After that, he lay in a hospital for a long time, unable to move any part of his body except his eyeballs. The woman he was married to at the time abandoned him and their two children. He was in this desperate situation when some Christians came to his hospital ward to pray for him and share the Gospel. Mr. Zhao regained his ability to sit up and move the upper half of his body, and through this miracle, he came to believe in Jesus. Early on, there were times he was so angry with God that he tore up his Bible and flung it to the floor. But in time, he had become a powerful witness for God and a man of noble character.

Because I was occupied and pressed by my graduation project, I was unable to take the post in the gallery in time, so I lost the opportunity. I suspect I might have been incompetent for the position anyway, for there were a lot of things inside me that needed to be dealt with. It was not that good luck never happened to me, but I had not developed the character to hold on to the blessings I received. I rarely contacted Mr. Zhao after our initial time together, for I knew he was a busy man and I was concerned he did not have time for fellowship with me. I thought of him often, though, and still do. The time I knew him was a special experience. The memory is still with me of how I was accepted as a brother in the Lord.

Before meeting Mr. Zhao, I had almost become convinced Betty and Tom were right. But through the experience of my baptism, I started to accept myself.

CHAPTER 14

Beijing

In November 2008, I moved to Beijing. To avoid questions about a man with an identification card identifying him as a woman, Shao Han rented a room for me with her identification. Prior to my move, an Internet friend called Yao, who was also a trans man helped me get a job. I was to work in a shopping mall bar making and selling drinks such as milk tea, juice and milkshakes. Yao was a Beijing native, four years older than me, and the first trans man I ever met. He had already had gender confirmation surgeries done at 411 Hospital after he graduated from college. His identification had been changed and he lived the life he wanted. He had a decent job that he liked, a stable relationship with his girlfriend, and the acceptance of his family. He could also buy high quality testosterone pills from the andrology hospital as a male, and then I could buy them from him.

The day after I settled in Beijing, I went to my job interview. The next day, I started work. The bosses were three young people: a man and two women. Rumor among my co-workers was that the women were lesbian lovers.

I found no pleasure or value in this job beyond the wage, nor did I have any plans or ambition for a career. Concerned about trouble over my identification, I had given up on the idea of finding work at a decent company. A job had become simply something I had to do to provide the necessities of life. My mind was rarely on the work. I acted like a man who expected more out of life, yet I did not know what that might be.

My uniform was a t-shirt. I had never worn a t-shirt in public without a jacket over it. Though my breasts were not obvious, I worried if I stood up straight, they would be. So, all day long, I stooped and strained, which was tiring. Accustomed to the relaxed lifestyle typical of Chinese universities, and still feeling the after-effects of my depression, I was a little sluggish and often criticized for moving too slowly.

It was my first time working and living socially as a man. In this new city, with little need to show my identification, people automatically assumed I was a man based on how I looked, dressed, spoke and acted. I was such an ordinary man of inferior stature, girls were no longer curious about me and kept a proper distance. But I was able to live inconspicuously among men, though they had previously excluded me. Some guys would spread their arm over my shoulder and ask questions like, "Have you had a girl? Or are you a virgin?" One told he had just been circumcised and how much it cost. A married man confided about sex with his wife as casually as women talk to each other about their menses. I was happy to be taken into their confidence and enjoyed my new sense of belonging among them.

Until I moved to Beijing, everybody knew my story. I need not, and could not, hide. I had to play a role that contradicted my heart. In Beijing, I was able to live as myself, but I had to hide. There could be no more intimate friendships with girls. Relationships with boys had to be kept within limits so I would not be exposed. In China, it is common and innocent for people of the same sex to share a bed. Guest rooms are rare, so if a friend is coming for an overnight stay, he will typically share your bed. But, when a male friend proposed hanging out at my house for the night, I had to refuse, which surprised him. Protecting my identity left people with the impression I was aloof or too shy. I did not act or speak as a man normally did. They thought I was weird, somehow, although they could not tell what it was about me that was odd.

Most of my life, I had oppressed my nature and hid myself in a group I did not belong to, while being ostracized from the group I identified with. Now the chains were off and no one knew my history. I was like a prisoner just set free after having his hands and feet chained for years—at a loss over how to walk and puzzled by liberty. At the same time, I felt like a felon on the run, always afraid to be discovered, disclosed, rejected and captured. I tried to cast off these mental restrictions, but it was a process. It took longer than I expected to learn to interact with people naturally and confidently as a man.

I thought my secret was well hidden until the day one of my bosses asked to talk to me alone. Her name was Song. She was strong and tall and had a short, masculine haircut. To my surprise, Song was a trans man. He knew of my circumstances from the beginning, because he was acquainted with Yao. Song told me he had already had top surgery in a private clinic that charged him three times more than usual. They wouldn't risk doing it for less, in case there was any dispute later, because Song could not produce a certificate of mental examination from a qualified doctor. Therefore, it was unethical to remove healthy body parts. Seeing I was confused by the bulges on his chest, Song put his hand under his clothes and pulled out a bra. He patted his chest and it became flat as a plain.

"I have to wear this thing every day!" he explained. When he passed through the security inspection, men and women stood in separate lines. He was stopped by a worker there once and questioned.

"Are you a man or a woman?"

His face was obviously feminine, but his body, with its flat chest, resembled a man's. So, in order to avoid trouble, he maintained the image of a woman in public by wearing a bra. As for the woman who owned a share of the bar, yes, she was his girlfriend.

After working at the beverage bar for a couple of weeks, I was politely fired by Song's girlfriend. I was unfit for the job, and she may have also felt it was unsafe to have someone around who knew their secret. Either way, it was a relief to me.

Meanwhile, I could not afford the little room in central Beijing. Although it was less than eight square meters, rents were soaring. So, after only one month, I moved to a basement in the Wangjing area, which is in the northeast within the fifth ring of the city. Because the rents were cheap, basements were full of *beipao*—Beijing drifters. Beipao lived and worked in the city without a permanent residence. Most struggled to make a living and had to move from time to time. Almost every Beijing transient has some bitter memory of their days in the basements.

The basements were usually part of residential compounds. Above the ground stood tall modern buildings with bright, shiny windows. There, the rich lived comfortable lives. Below ground lay large labyrinths of rooms where the poor lived. To reach them, one went through a ground level entrance and down stairs. The sunlight would become dimmer and dimmer until it was replaced by the pale yellow light of bulbs installed along the passage walls. Rooms sat side by side along the corridor. The noise of water running in the public bathrooms echoed through this tunnel from time to time.

The room I rented was about eight square meters. There was nothing inside except one small, old bed against the mottled wall and a shabby side table. The floors were cement, which was cold and damp. In this den, it was impossible to see if it was day or night. It was completely dark when the light was off. Only clattering from the drain that went through the room broke the silence once in a while.

I was worried about registering for the room, so I asked the janitor if Shao Han could register for me. He said no. I told him my identification was lost, but wrote down my name and identification card number for him.

Later, while Shao Han and I were cleaning up the room, the janitor came to see me.

"I checked this ID. Why is it female? Is that ID your sister's?" he asked, for he thought Shao Han was my sister.

"No," I said, without thinking.

Fortunately, he did not press the matter, although he was suspicious of me. Maybe because the Olympics were over he didn't need to be so strict and didn't want to lose a tenant.

After I settled in the basement, I found a job as an assistant in another gallery in the 798 Art District. Because of the financial crisis in 2008, Mr. Zhao had suffered losses and withdrawn his gallery from "798."

When the boss requested a copy of my identification, I didn't feel I could trust her with the truth as I had Mr. Zhao. There were some people I did not trust, so I never revealed anything to them. I had worked quite a few days by the time she asked for my identification, and had acted instinctively as a man. I was skeptical she would accept me after she knew I was transsexual. I was disturbed. Thinking of how the janitor had looked suspiciously at me, I decided my story of the lost identification sounded far-fetched. So, I resorted to a fake identification card.

Advertisements for fake certificates appeared everywhere in Beijing: on bus stops, streets and in every corner of the city. On my day off, I visited a nearby neighborhood and dialed one of the numbers painted on a wall. Soon, a woman on a bike appeared at the appointed place. She took me to the local photo studio to have my picture taken.

"Just have the gender changed, that's all," I requested.

She found that amusing and laughed, but she did not question me. She did not doubt I was a man, nor did she care as long as she got her profit. Hours later I paid her 80 yuan and she handed me a fake identification card along with my real one. When I gave the counterfeit to my boss, she believed it was authentic. Ironic, since when I showed my real identification card, people said it was false.

Sometime later, the boss mentioned she planned to attend a fair being held in Shanghai. I was to go along. Again, I was troubled, thinking of the inconvenience of lodging in a hotel. I would have to share a room with another man and who knew what would arise involving identification. What if my fake identification did not work? I was so worried that I resigned after three months.

I needed to find something I could do on my own to make a living. One option was to work as a "witkey" online. Witkeys are freelancers who offer services through online platforms. Certain websites help employers and freelance workers find each other. The projects are mostly graphic design work, such as posters, business cards, and logos. Sometimes there are translations jobs, too. If my work was selected from among all the entries, I would be paid. If not, I labored in vain. So, I tried to learn graphic design by myself and be a witkey.

In retrospect, I don't remember many specifics during my time in the basement. Those days were pale, bitter and gloomy. I would never again live in a windowless room like an ant in a subterranean colony. Who in that city knew or cared that I existed there? Shao Han's weekend visits were my only comfort. I had very few possessions and her love was the only one of any value. But how long could it be sustained under the circumstances?

CHAPTER 15
Disillusioned with Love

In May 2009, I moved to an apartment on the twentieth floor of another residential compound. Shao Han dealt with the house agent alone and signed the contract, so there were no worries about my identification. The apartment was divided into many rooms by partitions. The kitchen and bath were public. Shao Han and I each rented a small room. My room was a little space partitioned from the big living room. Hers had a window with a broad view. The house was brand new and we were the first tenants.

When we got the keys and stepped into the bright, clean house where fresh air flowed freely, we imagined for a moment we had just bought the house. Such a big, nice house was beyond the financial ability of a Beijing drifter. In fact, the annual wages of an average worker would not be enough to afford a space the size of a bathroom in this house, but for a little while, it was all ours.

Soon, various people moved into the house, putting an end to our fantasies. One was an ambitious young man who worked in the BMW sales department. Another was a tall bill collector who looked ferocious. He brought with him a diminutive wife and a gang of fellows. There was also a rich man in his thirties who stayed home most of the time while his lover—a young woman with a mysterious job—worked nights, and a plain girl who lived next to Shao Han.

Most of the day, I sat before my computer in my small room and browsed the witkey sites for feasible projects. I was not professionally trained, so my work was slow, but I did it with all my heart to add to its chances of being selected. This work came with no guarantees, like gambling. My chips were my time and energy. After a loss, I told myself to try one more time, hold on, maybe I would win the next one. I did succeed once, the first and only time I tried for a translation job: about 1,000 words from Mandarin to English. I found that so ironic. Looking back, I probably should have changed my focus immediately. One way or another, months of this risk ended with me running out of money after making less than 100 yuan altogether.

Always broke, I ate only bread or just drank water to alleviate my hunger. Unable to meet my basic needs, I fell into a bad mood. I felt trapped and sometimes couldn't bear to stay in my room any longer, so I wandered the streets with no direction. One day, I saw a pedestrian pick up her dog to cross the street and found myself envying the dog. It was better off than I was in those days.

Shao Han was pricked by another kind of thorn. Every day, she woke up to the noise of her alarm, set out early to catch the company bus, traveled more than an hour, and sometimes had to work overtime. She often complained about how tired she was. She expected me to cook and have dinner ready when she got home from work, but came back to find only a cold pan. I added to her pressure when I couldn't pay my entire rent. Now and again, problems popped up with her old apartment, which was sublet. I was unable to shield her or understand the difficulties she encountered in her work. Han said frankly she wanted a mature man, which I was obviously not, and wondered why I would not simply go to work.

"How long have you been resting?" she demanded. "If you can't find a career, at least you could be a dishwasher in a restaurant."

The word "resting" was a dagger to me and I was still very focused on myself. "How can I work in a company as a woman?" I answered back. "Which bathroom should I go in? How will they see me?"

"So what? You care about it too much. I also want to hide in a shell and stay home every day, but I don't."

I was too ashamed to face her, but Shao Han interpreted my lack of response differently. "I move about right before your eyes every day, but you don't treasure me," she said.

I was struck dumb. I did not know how to respond to her disappointment and displeasure. Little by little, she let me know she was leaving me. I had nothing to offer her and no way to reassure her about a future with me.

"You must get rich," she told me, "so that my family will accept you and disregard your shortcomings. Yet, you are not even able to guarantee my basic life needs."

I did try to find a job afterwards. It was becoming a matter of survival, so I set aside my misgivings. I sent out my resume online and visited print shops in person, but got no reply or was rejected. Finally, a company gave me a try, but after one day of probation, they decided not to hire me. Another printing company hired me and fired me after one week because I failed to complete the work I promised. A church was looking for an usher, but they said I looked too forlorn for the position.

Shao Han was from a close-knit family. It amazed me that a mother and her child called each other so frequently. For them, it was just normal. In order to conceal her relationship with me, Shao Han had to lie when her mother asked questions like: "Where are you?" "What are you doing?" "Who are you with?" Shao Han was tired of the deception. Meanwhile, her mother could not bear to see Shao Han living a lonely, hard life in Beijing.

Every time she came home from a visit, Shao Han would say, "My mom wants me to go back to Shijiazhuang and I also hope to live close to them and honor them. They brought me up, but I have done nothing to repay them yet."

In September, Shao Han resigned. Her mother had paved the road for her to go home by procuring a position for Shao Han in a state-owned enterprise close to their house.

Shao Han did what she could for me before she left. She cleared my computer to make it run faster. She was good at that. She bought me an electric kettle for boiling water and a green potted plant. She accompanied me to rent another room in a village called Dongxindian, helped pack and move my belongings, and settled me into my new lodgings. She sublet the two rooms on the twentieth floor. Han was outgoing, able to deal with any kind of person freely, and did all these things with competence.

The last time we would share a bed, we woke in the morning light with Han nestled into my arms. She adjusted her body so she could have most of her back against me.

"If only I could perform a magic trick and shift you into the body of some man who lives in Shijiazhuang," she said.

"Then where would the man go?" I asked.

"Then he would disappear."

I imagined how it would be if I was the son of some average family in Shijiazhuang with a stable job. How Han and I would meet, date, start a relationship, visit each other's families. I would be introduced to her dad and mom, who Han had often described to me, and see their house, which she had illustrated for me on a piece of paper. We would eventually be engaged and married.

Han interrupted my fantasy, saying: "Maybe we didn't meet at the right time. Do you regret us? I don't regret us, anyway."

"I don't either," I said.

"When you prosper, please don't come back to me."

"Why?"

"Because I left you when you were poorest."

Would I ever prosper, I wondered. Was I cursed? But I did not say that aloud.

Knowing it was the last time we would ever snuggle like this, we both hoped to delay the hour when she had to get up. Her parents were arriving in Beijing early that morning; Han needed to pick them up from the station. They wanted to visit some places of interest in the city before returning home. Because the bed in the newly rented room was big enough for three people to sleep on, they were to spend several nights there, while I stayed in the room on the twentieth floor.

On September 24, 2009, at seven in the morning, I cooked a bowl of noodle soup—the last meal I would have in the apartment Shao Han and I had lived in since May. After breakfast, I was supposed to leave for the room in Dongxindian. Shao Han would soon be hours away by train. When Han and her parents came to move the luggage downstairs, I was eating noodles in the kitchen. Unusually, I had the door closed. Truthfully, I was hiding in there.

The sound of luggage being tugged across the floor made me nervous. I heard Han say to her father, "My classmate also lived here."

"Good, that's helpful," said a middle-aged male voice with an accent.

I stayed in the kitchen, as though there was danger outside, until the sounds ceased. I was certain Shao Han would come in to say goodbye. After a silent while, sure enough, she pushed through the door and immediately took hold of me. Automatically, I returned her embrace. She placed her chin on my shoulder, comfortingly.

"They are waiting downstairs," she said. "I am leaving. . .I'll be back in October. Take care!"

Suddenly, she gripped me so tightly she took a bite of my shoulder. Then, she turned and rushed downstairs. I stood there, motionless, for as long as the warmth of her body remained.

The violent pain in my shoulder would soon fade, but the hurt in my heart started to expand like cancer cells. It spread until the agony was everywhere at every moment. I walked out of the kitchen to Shao Han's empty room, stood by the window, and looked out from the twentieth floor. I could see the Shao family waiting with several packs of luggage by the roadside. A taxi stopped nearby and the Shaos loaded the large packs, one-by-one, into its trunk. Father Shao sat in front; Han sat in back with her mother. It seemed I could hear the driver ask them where to go and their answer: "Beijing West Railway

Station." Shao Han raised her right hand to grasp the door strap as the taxi moved away, faster and faster, farther and farther. When it disappeared around a turn, my heart wrung and a lump rose into my throat. I almost cried. Despite Han's promises to return, intuition told me this goodbye was forever.

At about nine o'clock that morning, I was in my newly rented room in Dongxindian preparing to set out for a job interview when three stern men in black shirts appeared at the door.

The foremost man had a file packet and asked firmly, "Are you Lei Jing?"

I nodded.

"Lock your door and follow us!"

I did and found a police car waiting for me downstairs. To the neighbors' and landlord's amazement, I got in. I was surprised and puzzled myself.

CHAPTER 16

In Lockup

A jail sat quietly in a certain corner of Chaoyang district of Beijing. Inside was a cell of about six square meters with dismal walls all around and a fearfully high ceiling. Way up on the wall was the only window: a small square, fenced with rust-stained bars. Through it, a bit of pale sky and thin branches could be seen, the songs of sparrows were heard, the cool and calming air blew, and the dim sunlight shone. On the wall opposite the window was a narrow, low door, also fenced with bars and a merciless big lock. No one knew where I was except the police and the guard who watched the outside door. My cell phone had been impounded, and I was shut into the cell before I could tell Shao Han or anybody. There was a dirty bunk along another wall and there I sat alone with the door on my left and the small, high window on my right.

I looked like a teenager, not fully grown, just taller than most girls. Lack of proper nourishment for a long time had made my arms and legs as thin as firewood. My skin was unhealthy and as gray as my life. The yellowing-white canvas shoes I wore had become dusty, and my dark gray pants were faded. An unbuttoned, black, short-sleeved shirt—fake Dior of good quality and simple style—covered my loose green undershirt. My hair was not nicely groomed; it had become rough and dry. Only my thick eyebrows shaped like swords and the sharp nose on my lean face showed any keenness. I kept my lips shut tightly, but I like to think my eyes were still bright and my overall demeanor demonstrated I was not a teenager.

I leaned forward, stoop-shouldered, hands folded, staring blankly at the opposite wall as though something could be seen through it. From time to time, I turned and looked up at the window, listening attentively to the tweet of the birds. The dim sunlight that filtered through the poor window was not enough to drive away the clamminess that penetrated my shoe soles and spread through my whole body. I stamped the muddy chipboard that covered the floor to keep my feet warm and rubbed my arms, but it was no use.

There was no sound except the sparrows. It seemed the policemen had gone all out to demonstrate their excellent work maintaining public order in light of the coming sixtieth anniversary celebration of the new China. There was only one guard sitting outside the jail. He looked like somebody's relative from the countryside, the kind of man who had not even finished middle school, so was introduced for the job. He wore a military jacket that was ridiculously large on him and sat there like a statue without thoughts, feelings, ambitions or visions. Though he was free, he looked restrained. Hearing my tramping, he asked that the chipboard be passed to him. When I requested the toilet, the guard unlocked the door and followed me, and then waited outside the washroom so he could return me to the cell promptly.

I was a person who tended to complain, to my family, society, and even God, but now, caught in this situation, I prayed instead. After a while, I seemed to have acquired some inner power to face anything. I did not know how much time had passed, but the light became dimmer and the room darker. I examined the stained mat I was sitting on. There were numerous faded red ink spots of blurred fingerprints on it, left by people who were once imprisoned. People were asked to press their inked fingertip on documents that charged them before they were put here. I had smeared mine on it too, moments after arriving.

How long must I stay here, I wondered. Will they set me free this evening? My fate was unpredictable. Time crept.

"September 24, 2009, what an impressive day!" I said to myself.

It was a day I will never forget, the day when I said farewell to my beloved Shao Han and then lost my freedom.

After the police car had carried me away from my rented room, the man sitting next to the driver had asked, "Lei Jing, where is your ID from? We checked online, there is no such person!"

I had no reply, needless to say. It was obvious the identification card was fake.

Days before, when I was moving some stuff into my new room, the landlord, a woman in her fifties or sixties, had come to see me.

"Young man, you must have a residence permit here. Please give me your ID and five yuan for the fee. I'll have it done for you at the local police station."

"Er, okay," I said, flustered. "I'll give it to you later."

Identification again. I shut the door behind me, struggling with which to give her, if I must surrender one. Han was leaving. I could not count on being shielded behind her this time. I dug my fake identification card out of a bag under the bed and scrutinized it.

Giving false identification was dangerous, but the potential embarrassment of being found out and considered female was unbearable to me. I could not stand to think of how people would stare at me. I went back and forth in my mind. "What shall I do?" I asked myself over and over. "Shall I risk giving her the fake one? Or risk being humiliated?"

My decision had landed me in a police car and, soon after, a police station. It wasn't until I was being interrogated that it dawned on them that the young man before them was actually a "girl"

"Are you 'T'? You are 'T', right?" one policeman asked insistently.

"Sorry, I don't know what 'T' is." I was confused. It seemed like a term for lesbian, but what did that have to do with me?

They went on with other questions. I confessed to everything: why, when, where, and how I had a fake identification. Seeing I meant no harm, they eased off and even showed a little sympathy for me. But, I had violated the law of the country and there must be a penalty. The charge was using false identification. I signed "Lei Jing" and pressed my fingerprint on the sheaf of papers they presented. Then, I was locked into a cell where I had plenty of time to consider how stupid it had been to present a fictitious identification to the police.

Night fell. Suddenly, the clatter of the lock turning in the steel door broke the silence.

"Come out!" yelled the guard.

I was escorted to another police car. The guard got in beside me. Where were they taking me? We traveled down a strange road flanked by streetlights that flamed like candle fires and left the rest of the world hiding in the dark. The car turned into the lane of a village and people gave way automatically. Some were walking leisurely with a bike, some were buying vegetables for dinner, some were rushing home from work. From inside the police car, it seemed like they were in another world. Next, we came to a wide, little traveled highway. A bus passing by seemed singular and lonely. It was packed with passengers. Their faces were expressionless, floating behind the windows like specters. The car finally stopped at a big steel gate in front of the vague outline of a dormitory building.

"Get out!" the guard ordered rudely.

He led me inside to a big, piercingly-illuminated square room. I was asked to sit and wait in one of the chairs lined up along a wall. In a second row of chairs, perpendicular to those I was in, sat a tame man in handcuffs. His feet were bare and dirty. I suspected he had resisted arrest, losing his shoes in the process. Policemen sat buried among papers at desks around the room. New "guests" were continually arriving and being taken away. A fat and wealthy looking man was removing his heavy gold necklace to be impounded, while nearby, a couple handed over their keys and wallets. An aged, bad-tempered man with a plastic bag of CT scans in one hand argued loudly with the police, demanding to be allowed to go home. A middle-aged woman was terrified of being put in jail. She resisted and wept like a child when she was dragged out. What a lively room!

After a long wait, I was summoned to the desk to sign and fingerprint more papers, and then handed to a guard who accompanied me to a physical examination.

When the guard saw the papers that charged me, he looked incredulous. "You are a woman?! You are a woman?!" I didn't reply.

First, I had to have a urine analysis. The toilet was in the corner of another room. It was just an open space with a few partitions. From the toilet where I stood, I could see the chairs along the opposite wall, which were full of people. I did not know what they were waiting for, but it seemed their minds were preoccupied with something, and nobody was paying attention to me. One way or another, I had to put a bold face on in that moment and carry the transparent plastic cup of urine across the room in front of all those people.

Then, I was taken to a room where there was only a young female working at a big machine. She had me stand on it, measured my height and weight, and took front and side portraits.

"Have you had any operations? Any scars on your body?" she asked in a voice that was as emotionless as her face.

"No."

"Remove your clothes."

"All of them?"

"Yes."

I had to switch my heart off, numb it to not feel, forget myself so I did not break down. I removed my shirt, vest, shoes and socks, unstrapped my belt, stripped off my pants, and finally stood naked before her. What powerful and hurtful proof that I had the body of a girl! I looked into a blank space to avoid seeing her or myself.

"Ok, put on your clothes."

In another room, I was given a blue and yellow suit and a pair of slippers. My own clothes and shoes were stored in a locker. Through the monitors in the room, I could see prisoners in different cells. They were all wearing that same blue and yellow. I had to put on that large, fat suit too, because I was going to join them.

A woman in police uniform took me through door after door of steel bars, up and down stairs, and into a wide corridor with cells on both sides. She stopped at one of them, unlocked the steel-fenced door, and motioned me inside. Excitement arose as I entered.

"Look! There comes a handsome boy! How come a man has been put in here? Is it a mistake?" About a dozen women gathered around me and examined me from head to heel, chattering non-stop.

"Are you a man or a woman?"

"Why did they arrest you?"

"Even your voice sounds like a man!"

"If only she is a man! That would be great! Don't you like being hugged by a man?"

When their curiosity was satisfied, they left me alone sitting on something like a kang, although not heatable, for prisoners to sit and sleep on. It took up about half of the twenty square meter rectangular cell. The lights went out and a stout girl with short hair that had turned scruffy and oily fell sound asleep beside me. The foul smell of urine and sweat from the military quilts blew up my nose, but at least the suspense and isolation I had suffered in the first small cell was over. I could feel the warmth of human breath and fell asleep, hungry and exhausted.

Over the next four days, I must have read "Chaoyang District Detention Center" hundreds of times. It was printed on the backs of the jailers' uniforms. During dull moments, of which there were a lot, I would stare at those words and spell them out in my mind. Other times, I counted the few things in the room: the transparent glass that separated the toilet from everything else, the green mat on the floor, a camera, a loudspeaker, several tube lights on the ceiling, and some posters advertising the rules of conduct in the jail. Or, I paced, paused, and then raised my head to watch the little bit of sky visible through a fenced window.

To combat the tortuous crawl of time, prisoners shared their stories. Indignant petitioners complained of being wronged. Young prostitutes revealed candid details of their jobs. Haughty gamblers cursed the police. A devout Falun Gong practitioner discussed faith with me. An eighteen-year-old country girl, charged with stealing, clung to me and shared her private tale. An aged woman, who was given the privilege of lying down during non-sleeping times, due to her illness, lay still most of the time. One of the prisoners was a multimillionaire. Another, charged with gambling, was an officer in a state-owned enterprise.

A sophisticated-looking prostitute, who was a year younger than me, confessed she had a husband and son in her hometown. Her family did not know what she was really doing in Beijing; they simply expected her to bring gifts and money every Spring Festival when she visited them.

I recognized one of the prisoners, the woman who had cried so piteously when she was dragged in. Her house in the central business district of Beijing had been pulled down, but she had not received any compensation for its loss. So, she went to petition in Tiananmen Square and was charged with disturbing public order.

Another prostitute was only seventeen, but already quite experienced. Most of the time, she just sat calmly. She ate only a bun at mealtimes, when she ate at all. But, she answered any questions put to her and once in a while volunteered a bit of her story. After she had quit middle school, a man seduced her with kindness and treats, finally persuading her to give herself willingly to him. Then he took her to Beijing to be a prostitute. He had done the same to many girls, whom he now controlled. Despite all this, she did not hate him and believed he would think of a way to get her out of prison. The rest of us did not think he would. It was the second time she had been caught, so a harsh sentence was likely waiting for her.

"If I am sentenced to a half year in the labor camps," she said, "I will commit suicide, for by the time I am out, I will be eighteen, and that's too old."

It seemed that, besides prostitution, she did not know what she could do to earn her living. She was so young—still a child fond of sweets—but she did not know how to value herself properly.

When we tired of talking, sitting and walking, we thought a great deal of time had passed, but that turned out to be only an illusion. A day seemed as long as a year. I thought of Han sometimes and felt an invisible knife cutting the days with her away from my life for good.

On the morning of September 29, I was led back through a series of doors and guards. When the last small door opened and closed behind me, I found myself standing in a bleak lane where some people were wandering and waiting for their friends or relatives to be released from the jail. Fortunately, I had some change in my pocket, which I used for bus tickets back to Dongxindian. I rode home with my eyes glued to the window, eager for the site of buildings, stores, billboards, streets and pedestrians, as if it was my first time seeing them.

Back in my room, it turned dark when I pulled the curtain, then I tucked myself into bed. Conditioned to the smelly quilt in the jail, I found it odd that the bedclothes I slept with everyday had so little scent. I burrowed into them like a frightened woodland creature going to ground and huddled soundlessly in their familiar depths. Spare me this moment of rest, undisturbed, I prayed. Allow me to lie here doing nothing. When I have gathered my strength, I will rise and rejoin the world. But for this moment, please leave me alone.

I switched on my phone, which I had just gotten back from the police. Shao Han had sent messages asking what had happened to me. She was worried since she had lost contact with me so suddenly. Mom seldom called me, maybe one or twice a year, but she happened to call during the days I was confined. She must have called repeatedly, and the more she found the situation weird, the more she called. When I finally returned her call, her harsh voice sounded impatient and irritated.

"Where have you been? Why didn't you answer the phone? How many times have I called?" she pressed. It was not because she was concerned about me, so much, but the frustration of failing to reach me bothered her. I was not about to tell the truth and hear her caustic remarks: "It serves you right! It's stubborn of you to pretend to be a man!" Definitely I would not invite that.

"I went nowhere," I said carelessly.

"Nowhere?" She raised her voice to a higher pitch.

I thought, but didn't say, "Don't ask. Please leave me alone." But my silence would only make her more curious. I had to say something.

"Well, I spent a few days at a friend's house and forgot my phone at home. I just came back today." Finally, Mom let the matter go.

I wanted to see my family before I threw myself into finding a job in Beijing, because I had a feeling I would not go back to my hometown for years after that. So, I said, "I want to return home for a visit soon."

"Then come back," Mom said, casually.

CHAPTER 17

Reckoning with God

It was the middle of October when I returned to Dongxindian. Mom had given me sixteen hundred yuan and Shao Han left six hundred yuan for me in a drawer. That was all the funds I had for my new start. Poverty chased me like a bandit. In order to make a living, I would have to set aside my pride, venture forth, and put off the issue of identification as long as I could. I hoped to pay back Shao Han as soon as possible.

Dongxindian was a village in a suburb beyond the fifth ring of Beijing. It was full of provincials, who had brought prosperity to the locals: as long as they had houses to rent out, they were free from worries about food and clothing. The houses were tube-shaped, with three or four floors, simple and raw. Narrow iron staircases, which made a drumming sound when you stepped on them, ran up the outside of these houses. The rooms were usually less than ten square meters with only a bed, sometimes a table. There was a public basin on the stairway landing of every floor. The toilet was a barn, like the one at my high school, but much smaller. A chamber pot was a necessity, and every morning you would see people carrying small red or green buckets filled with the night's bodily waste, which needed to be dumped.

Once, as I walked into the barn, I accidentally saw a man's private parts while he was taking a squat. Then I realized it was not safe for me to go to this kind of men's room. I could not pee standing up. I had to pretend to take a squat so other men in the barn wouldn't start wondering about me. Seeing that man's genitals hanging causally beneath him as he squatted made me realize my toileting theatrics were not enough to protect my secret. So, I had a big problem, for our house had no indoor bathroom. But how long can one manage without access to a toilet? I soon learned, and I hope I never have to live that way again.

The streets of Dongxindian were jammed. There was always a stream of pedestrians hurrying to and fro on the bumpy road, mostly young people or graduates who worked in the city. During rush hour, they marched so quickly one had to dash to keep up. If you slowed down, someone behind you would walk on your heel. At the bus station on the highway, commuters pressed into a great mass. Their heads bobbed and craned to see if the next bus was theirs. If it was, they scrambled and pushed onto the already crowded motor coach. What made people live this kind of life, I wondered. I imagined each had some belief or dream that kept them in Dongxindian. I had originally come for love, after all. But now that my love was gone, I stayed only because I did not know anywhere else I could go.

I did not have any substantial work experience, although I had graduated a year previously, which complicated my job prospects. I browsed listings on recruitment websites, sent out resumes, made phone calls asking for an interview if I thought a position was feasible, and ran about to job fairs. Once, a woman standing at a job fair booth said, "Sorry, we have no positions for males," before I had even come close enough to make an inquiry. That made me realize it was no longer possible for me to work as a female, even though I had decided I would bear it if necessary. Another time, I went for an interview and decided to tell the truth. At first, the two interviewers treated me well and seemed to have a good impression of me. Then I showed them my diploma. I said nothing but pointed to the character "female." They stared at each other and at last said, "We need to consider this and we will call you." I knew it was just a mild rejection.

On November 1, 2009, the first snowfall in Beijing signaled the start of winter, but to keep from missing an interview, I ventured out. The snow blotted the sky and earth so thickly I could hardly open my eyes or take a step. My head was covered in snow and soon drenched. The position was house agent, so the entrance hurdle was low. I had been frustrated so many times, I accepted the job without thinking too much.

While working as a house agent that winter I was caught a few times in heavy snow, got my hair drenched, walked until I was weary, and sometimes took a super-crowded bus home. Finally, I fell sick. That night, I turned the light off early, needing sleep. I huddled down into my bed, which was close to the heater, but it was useless. I felt cold all the same and could not stop shivering. Physically, I was exhausted, but my brain was wide awake, so I could not sleep. I had no strength to cry aloud to God, only a small internal voice.

Thinking of the possibility of the deadly H1N1 influenza virus, I was glad. I imagined myself lying in the isolation ward, dying a lonely death, saying goodbye to this desperate life. I knew my time was in God's hands and such a good thing might not befall me so young, but I was not afraid of death. It seemed easier than living. I was only afraid I was not qualified to stand before God if I died just then.

Except vomiting, I exhibited all the early symptoms of H1N1. I coughed so hard my belly ached. Sometimes I shivered and sometimes I had spasms of fever. It was hard to breathe in the cold air. My eyes burned and my throat was sore. My body felt powerless and like I was floating. My muscles hurt, I had diarrhea, and my brain seemed to collapse. All of a sudden, I had forgotten a lot of English words.

I missed Shao Han during every empty moment. We called one or two times at first, and chatted online, but she had turned more and more aloof, stopped responding, and finally deleted me from her friends list. I knew she was a logical person. Once she made a decision, she acted on it in a level-headed way, and now she was determined to forget me. No matter how much I missed her, I must control myself and not contact her so I could forget her, too. However, during my illness, she was the only person I could think of. I kept expecting she would send me a surprise text message. Hungry for her comfort, I dialed her number and listened nervously to the line beeping, but then hung up. I didn't call again. I missed her terribly, but I knew my yearning for her actually had nothing to do with her anymore. What I needed was to deal with my own feelings. In my diary, I wrote:

So close are you in my memory,

Yet so far in reality,

Even if you emerge right now before me,

You are as distant as a stranger,

For our hearts do not run along the same track any longer.

Over the course of that year, my relationship with Shao Han, which had represented all God was to me, had died. I had weakened, failed, become discouraged, and fell ill. Finally, family, friends, my lover, money, health, and physical comfort, all receded and I found myself in an emotional wilderness inhabited only by the Almighty and me. He tugged at my heartstrings and opened my eyes. In sorrowful amazement, I saw the truth about myself. I had been self-righteous, believing that my parents and the world owed me something. With indifference and hatred filling my heart, I had surmised myself a justified victim. I had wallowed in self-pity that prevented me from seeing anything but my own pain.

I thought of the friends whom I had treated rudely, hanging up on their calls and ignoring their encouraging messages. I hadn't had the sense to appreciate others' kindness. And how selfish I had been toward Qingqing! My motives had been evil. I had only sought the pleasure of possessing her and had never intended to commit to her. If a new girl had come along, I would have forsaken Qingqing in an instant. How I must have hurt her. What a sorry thing to do!

During my relationship with Shao Han, I had ignored my responsibilities, letting things drift and slide. I had dishonored marriage with her, made her my idol, and placed her on a throne. I had depended on her as the determining factor of my happiness, satisfaction and hope, though she was only mortal.

When I worked for the printing company, I had not kept my word and had been negligent in my duties. I refused to face my fears, hid in my shell, and idled. Realizing how I had acted left me feeling ashamed, regretful and sad beyond description.

I asked God for his mercy again, but this time, not because of my transsexualism. For once, my body seemed beside the point. I asked for grace because I was a helpless, sinful person and I had been ignorant of it.

I felt I could see God waiting for me to repent and he showed me he loved me, despite my unworthiness. It was as if I could hear him whisper, "Your spirit is dead, though your body is alive. You are like a corpse giving off the foul odors of bitterness, pride, self-righteousness and indulgence in self-pity. But see? I have removed the stone from your grave and given you new life, just as I raised Lazarus from the dead. You thought you would be happy if only you had the surgeries, if only you found your true love, if only you reached the other side of your troubles. What you are really in want of is wisdom. Without the wisdom of how to deal with money, you will not be happy, even if you become a millionaire. Without the wisdom of how to manage marriage, you will not be happy, even if you succeed in marrying a woman you love. Without the wisdom of how to live well, you will not be happy, even if you find harmony between your body and soul. You have made many things your idols, believing you would be happy if you got them. They have been your focus, the beneficiaries of all your energy. You have been consumed and suffered for them willingly, foolishly and in vain. You were so obsessed with these illusions, your eyes were blocked and your heart was captivated. But now your idols are broken and you have lost everything you loved. Now look to me: the way, the truth, and the life."

I had believed the disagreement between my body and soul was the root of all my troubles. I had taken no responsibility for my part in my predicament. I had not trusted the Lord to help me overcome my agony. But I came to understand at the end of that hard year, that even if my body had matched my soul, there could be little happiness as long as I remained mentally immature and deficient in character. Though it was difficult to discover and acknowledge my flaws, it was necessary. God was doing restorative work inside of me. He had torn and he healed. He injured and he bound up. He did not operate on my body, but on my soul.

I decided it was time to grow up, but soon learned that was easier said than done. I quit the house agent job and ended up working for a small foreign trade company. I found the position through a Christian recruitment website. The boss was Christian, a single woman around forty-years-old. She perceived I was in financial difficulty and paid me in advance to tide me over. She never asked for my identification until I left. The company was in an apartment she rented in the sixth ring on the east side of Beijing. She lived there as well. The living room served as the office. There were two workers, me and a young mother. The company also ran a factory located in a village outside the sixth ring. I went back and forth between the office and factory every day, and often joined the factory workers when they were short-handed. Our main product was salt lamps.

When working at the factory, there was no difference between me and a rural laborer. I smelt earthy and was covered with dust from head to heel. My clothes felt rough and so did my hair and fingers. The back of my hands were like bark. The sleeves and the front part of my work jacket had worn shiny, and my gloves had holes. Sometimes my head ached as if there was a nail in it because of the carbon monoxide emissions that came from the stove next to where I worked. The whole winter I wore one pair of canvas shoes and a military-green coat. I didn't have extras to change into.

The workers in the factory were mostly uneducated country women. There was a girl younger than twenty working there with her mother. She had not even finished primary school. We often worked together assembling, packing and binding. She once asked me, "Since you went to college, why are you working in such a place?"

I might have felt humiliated before, but I was not stung by her words. I had decided that whatever I could do, I would do it, no matter how lowly the work. There was nothing to complain about, it was just what I deserved. I would do what I was to do, bear what I was to bear, and somehow alleviate my regret over the past. And, I tried to find the value in the work. In the dusty, smoke-filled storehouse, I acquired an understanding of how people cooperated to get things done, how information was communicated, how a product was made, how a boss made use of money to keep all of this happening, and how to respond and stay unaffected when people said things that were offensive.

Outside, the sky was pastel in harmony with that austere winter. Occasionally, a flock of birds passed over as I gazed up. It seemed the past had slipped away on the wind as well. I could not believe it was only three months since Shao Han left. It seemed like three years. She had weathered in my memory to a blurry outline without flesh and blood.

Work could temporarily occupy my mind, despite the physical discomfort, but sometimes I was left alone in the office when the boss and my co-worker went out together. With only the sound of typing, time dragged. I could not continue anything and could not find anyone to talk to. I had all these thoughts and feelings from the past, present and future that I needed to vent, but no one I could turn to for help. Oh, I wanted to be spoken to. I longed for the warmth of human companionship. I paced the floor, but that was of no use. When the day turned dark, I inserted myself into a bus full of people, yet none of them were related to me. I would have been satisfied holding a stray dog, just so long as I could feel another living creature.

December was severely cold. The water froze at the tap. The plant Shao Han had left me, unable to survive the cold, had rotted. In my little room, permeated with loneliness, my soul felt like it had been drenched in cold water. The room was so quiet I could hear my heart throbbing. Why did it still beat? Death would be easier. If only I had a right to end my life. A bowl of porridge was my dinner. I cried soundlessly as I had a spoonful. I only ate it because I knew I had to live.

I hoped God was hearing my prayers and seeing my tears, as promised in Isaiah 38:5. "Strengthen me and uphold me," I pled, whenever my determination seemed likely to fail me that hard winter.

At the end of the bystreet where I lived was a steep slope. A railway crossed the slope and there was a poplar wood to one side. During that dreary era of my life, my favorite thing was to take a walk along the track, leaving the bustle of the city. Far from the maddening traffic and crowds, I could gain a little mental space, slow my steps, reflect and forget the bitterness of my situation temporarily. It was there I watched the tail of 2009 finally vanish with the coming of the new year.

In the pale winter sun, with the wind blowing upon my face, I walked the tracks, which extended out of sight into the distance. Without buildings blocking my view, I could see as far as I wished with my physical and spiritual eyes. Standing at the starting line of 2010, I believed the worst was past and life would be better in the coming year.

"May I do away with the old and be a new creation in Christ," I prayed.

CHAPTER 18

Guangzhou

One day around the time of the Lantern Festival, a white car stopped at the factory just at closing time. Two women got out of the car. They had a substantial look and were obviously of a superior class. The taller woman especially attracted me. She looked to be in her forties and was very elegant and good looking. Her dress was not so feminine, but high-grade, and she looked modern with a pair of sunglasses pinning her hair back from her forehead. Her high straight nose, slightly knit brows, and determined air, rendered her stately, but she was affable when she talked and her Mandarin was very pleasant to hear. I could not help wondering who she was, what career she engaged in, and what property she possessed.

I received the two women in dirty, dusty clothes with a hood covering half my face, but they did not despise me for my terrible appearance. I served them as best I could, displayed and demonstrated the lamps, and then loaded their order into the car trunk.

When the elegant woman pressed the button to start her car, it did not work. She tried a few times in vain and then came to suspect there was a problem with the battery in her key. It was dark and cold and the women were in a hurry to leave. So, the elegant woman turned to me.

"Young man, could you do me a favor and buy a battery for me?" she asked. "I am a stranger here."

I considered it my honor and hurried to a nearby store. Once the new battery was installed, the car started. Then, to my surprise, the elegant woman rolled down her window.

"Would you like to go to Guangzhou and work there?" she asked.

I was elated. "Yes!" I answered without hesitation. I had been praying for a better job. If there was anywhere I could go to get one, I would go.

The elegant woman told me her phone number and name—here I will call her Ms. Wu—and said, "Send me your resume." It sounded like she was ready to hire me!

With high hopes, I did send my resume, but the weeks of silence that followed made me think she wasn't serious after all. I put the episode out of my mind until one day in April. I was running errands outside when I received a call from Ms. Wu. She said she was in Macao and would like to meet with me when she came to Beijing the next week. I could not believe it.

The next Saturday, as I waited for her in the lodge of the downtown residential compound where she lived, I noticed that whenever a car passed through the entrance, the driver would glance at me. The elderly gatekeeper told me many celebrities lived in that compound, including Lui Huan, the famous singer who performed in the opening ceremony of the Beijing Olympics, and Pu Cunxi, the actor. They greeted the gatekeeper every day. I was amazed to learn this and then understood why the residents of the compound were looking at me.

During my talk with Ms. Wu, she revealed she was an actress. She'd had some fame in the 1980s, had worked with the influential director, Xie Jin, was acquainted with some famous people, and had won a Golden Rooster award for best supporting actress. She had withdrawn from acting and ran a company that trained child performers. Her company was in Guangzhou, and she wanted me to be her assistant there. She said buying car batteries would not be part of my job description, but she had been touched by my actions, and she wanted her staff to adopt the same high standards of service. I accepted her offer happily.

Although my boss at the salt lamp company would have liked me to stay, she did not try to prevent me from resigning.

"If you find it is not good there, you are welcome back anytime," she said.

I packed my belongings and consigned my luggage. The preparations went so smoothly and with such perfect timing, I believe God must have approved of my decision. In one week, I was on the train to Guangzhou. Before I left Beijing, I finished paying Shao Han the money she had spent on me, which was more than due.

As the train moved out of Beijing, variegated flowing images flashed past the window, brilliant in the light of dusk, and fragments of memory flickered in my brain.

"Goodbye, Beijing. I don't belong to you and you don't belong to me," I said softly. The past moved away from me as I traveled further away from the north. I was heading to the south that I had looked toward from the top of the hill in my hometown when I was young. Life there was totally unknown. I had fears and worries, but I wanted to embrace a brand new life and I was convinced God was with me. I was sure that I would be secure in the south, and this move had been engineered by his invisible, mighty hand.

I arrived in a peaceful, beautiful community surrounded by water and settled into an apartment the company rented as a dormitory. There were other male workers sharing the houses, but fortunately, I had a small, private bedroom. Finally, the troubles of toileting and bathing were over, but there was one thing I hadn't reckoned on— the southern climate.

The heat of Guangzhou is oppressive. One may as well be living in a food steamer. The heat invades from everywhere, stinging like thousands of needles. Where I grew up in the north, the weather was never hot to such an extent. In Guangzhou, one often could not fall asleep at night and the brain could not function. Sweat would roll off my forehead in big drops that soaked my eyes. Water came burning from the tap.

In Guangzhou, men stripped to the waist, wearing only underpants when indoors handling everyday concerns. I worried my dorm mates found it queer that I always wore an undershirt, no matter how hot it was. I stopped putting on two layers, as I had in the north. That would make me too eccentric, as if I felt cold. Wearing one layer of shirt turned out to be fine, for I was thin and the bulges on my chest were not so obvious as long as I avoided standing too straight. Still, this made me anxious and tired of always trying to disguise something. So, I seldom joined the other men in activities or conversations and spent most of my time in my room with the door closed. Consequently, the other men considered me abnormally unsocial.

At least they did not doubt my identity. For most people, transsexuality was only a novelty reported by the media. People did not expect a transsexual person to be living right under their noses, so nobody associated my odd behaviors with gender issues. Still, in Guangzhou, top surgery became more pressing and urgent.

In 2005, a transman named Gengzi finished his gender confirmation surgeries at Guangzhou Armed Police Hospital and became the first openly transsexual man in China. In the summer of 2010, I appeared at the same hospital. A thirty-something female doctor from the plastic surgery department received me, her voice and expression full of contempt. She read aloud the conditions I would have to meet coldly, as if she was trying to frighten me away. I was not dissuaded. The doctor went to talk to her friend, another woman wearing a white gown, which was a hint for me to leave.

Truly, the medical and legal barriers are high. In China, hospitals are not allowed to do sexual reassignment surgeries unless the patient has been certified transsexual by a mental specialist, but such specialists are so rare no one even knows whom to turn to. On my way out, I saw there was a psychology department at the hospital, so I went there and registered, explaining I needed a certificate for gender confirmation surgery.

"So you are a man and you want to be a woman?" asked the doctor, an elderly woman sitting behind her desk. I almost burst into laughter.

After learning the reverse was true, the doctor was terrified and believed I was incurable. She said she was not competent to take on such a case and sent me away immediately, without charging her usual fee.

Once again, I turned to the web for access to information. In November of 2010, I learned about testosterone injection on an Internet chat room. Trans men on the forum had shared the effects testosterone injection had on their bodies. In addition to masculinizing physical appearance, they reported it would stop menstruation. I was immediately ready to do whatever it took to get the injections.

Injectable testosterone is a prescription drug, but without access to appropriate medical care, my only choice was to find it on the black market. Fortunately, everything is available on the Internet. I did some research and found only one brand of injectable testosterone available in China. After some more research, I located a credible online seller. They were asking 30 yuan per dose then—the price is higher now and will continue to rise—but how does one really count the cost of integrating body and soul? I started purchasing a dozen injections once a year and have injected once a month since.

The clinics wouldn't inject for me unless I could present a prescription from a doctor, so I resorted to the Internet again. I ordered hypodermic needles and studied the procedure for intramuscular injection.

Before injecting the first time, I examined the little seamless glass bottle. I wasn't even sure how to open it. I resorted to using a compass to break the neck of the bottle. Shattered glass flew to the floor, but I managed not to spill any of the precious liquid inside. After drawing the fluid with an injector, I rubbed medical alcohol on my lateral thigh, above the knee. I wished my eyes could penetrate the surface of my skin and help me avoid those invisible blood vessels that lay beneath it. Without a doctor to guide me, I did not know the specific dangers of hitting a vein, only that it was a bad thing to do.

The moment the needle tip pierced my skin, it hurt so much I flinched and lost my grip on the injector. I knew I could not stop at the surface, but as the needle went deeper, the sting became fiercer.

Despite the pain, an irresistible power drove me on. I was no different than any other suffering patient who has made the decision to do whatever was necessary to find a cure. I was willing to go to any length, try every known method, even if the treatment tortured me. Sometimes, the cure hurts, yet people subject themselves to chemotherapy, catheters, knives, needles—any kind of pain—for the promise of healing.

Finally, I could not bear it any longer and stopped again. For quite a while I did not have the nerve to draw the needle out, nor push it in deeper. At last I gave up and withdrew it. Blood came out immediately. I had hit a vein.

Unwilling to give up, I tried my left arm. I slipped the metal bevel under my skin once again, and then, with a slight sound like that of a needle pushed through cloth, it pierced my muscle and I was able to bury it properly. The angle required made it hard for me to push the plunger with enough force, and sweat from my fingertips made the injector slippery, but I managed to press the oily fluid into my muscle. A fresh sting passed through my nerves, but once I became conditioned to the pain, it did not seem unendurable. I tried to relax my arm, but my efforts were complicated by the trembling in my right hand. I felt hot all over and kept my eyes fixed on the scale printed on the barrel of the syringe. Milliliter by milliliter the fluid drained until, finally, the last drip disappeared and I could remove the needle. I circled the date on my calendar as a reminder to repeat the same scene in a month.

A hard bulge had developed at the injection site as the liquid seeped into my arm. I didn't know if that signaled a problem or if it was normal. I was never sure my technique was correct. Sometimes there was a great deal of pain, sometimes not. Sometimes the injection site bled, sometimes not. But, it worked.

After a couple of months, my menses finally stopped for good. Initially, I gained weight again, but after a few months of regular injections, my weight dropped back to normal and has remained stable ever since. The oily chemical liquid shaped my body from the inside out so that I presented with typical male features: my legs grew hairy, my Adam's apple protruded, my face became more angular, and for the first time a beard appeared on my chin, though it was sparse. My muscle distribution shifted and the fat on my thighs diminished. My hips turned narrow and my waist strong. In addition to injecting myself with testosterone, I jogged and lifted weights to enhance my male presentation.

I am very happy with these changes, despite the pimples I get from the testosterone and my concerns for my overall health. I have no idea if the testosterone injections are causing internal damage and few options for finding out. China has no special medical care facilities for people who are transsexual.

Why would I spend so much money and take such chances to interfere with the development of my female body? Why was I so happy to appear as a male, though imperfectly? All I can say is that something in my nature drives me. I have a need to have a male body that allows me to live authentically as I am internally. I cannot rest until my body is in the form that matches my soul, even if it means self-destruction. This need is so real, so strong, and so irresistible all I can do is bow to it.

There are some who believe it is sinful for a man like me to forcibly and artificially alter a healthy body granted by Heaven. If that is true, may God have mercy on me and all the people like me, for we cannot help ourselves. But, if what I believe is right, if I am truly a man, may God have mercy on me and all the people like me, for we are only doing our best to live as He created us, yet the majority persecute us.

CHAPTER 19

Mr. Ray

Every step of transition comes with its own set of new challenges. One day while I was working, the phone rang.

"Hello."

"Hello."

"Er. . .this is Lei Jing's number right?" a man's voice said hesitantly.

"Uh. . .yes." I had almost forgotten I used to be called Lei Jing. Who could this be calling my phone?

"May I speak to her?" the man asked. "I am her uncle."

"I'm. . .she," I admitted.

"But. . .it's a man's voice!"

The last time I had seen this uncle, my father's brother, was in 2003 when my grandmother passed away. He was calling from Shenzhen. He had learned from Dad that I was in Guangzhou, quite close to him. My uncle was calling to invite me to visit him. Despite his confusion over my voice, he told me enthusiastically where he lived, how to get there, and the day he would be free.

For a stranger in a strange place, it should be great to have a relative to visit, but my uncle would expect a girl's figure to appear on his door step. Even if I was standing right before him, he would wonder where his niece was. I did not go.

For three years, I avoided family as I worked to build a normal, stable life. My new job complicated things. It turned out the company I was working for did not operate on regular hours or with much discipline. There were no clear boundaries about when to work and when to rest. It was like being a servant who must wait for orders twenty-four hours a day and had no freedom or privacy. Dissatisfied, I quit after four months and found a job as an assistant teacher in a Christian school in the neighborhood. This did not end my good relationship with Ms. Wu. She found me trustworthy and had me work for her now and then in my free time.

The day before classes commenced, a staff meeting was held and we were told every teacher must have a body-check. I was dismayed. How would the body checks be done? Individually or in groups? Would identification be required? What parts of the body would be checked? Would I be exposed in front of other teachers?

I learned I could go to the neighborhood clinic by myself and would receive a results form I could turn in to the school. Not knowing what to expect from the examination, I was still worried, but what choice did I have except to try? One early morning, I reported to the clinic and sat at the desk of a doctor who asked for basic information and filled in a form quickly without raising her head. I saw her check the box for "M" in the gender section of the form. People will ask your name or age, but few will ask your gender. We judge for ourselves based on what we hear or see in a person, rather than respecting the will of the person being identified. However, most of the time, our assumptions are correct. Seeing that "M," I felt there was nothing to be nervous about until cold metal touched the skin on the left side of my chest.

"Hm. Your heartbeat is a little fast," the doctor remarked. I was thankful she didn't have an instrument that could read my mind.

Next, I was required to hand over copies of my certificates. I had prepared for this moment by scanning my certificates into a computer and editing the images with Photoshop. I only changed one character on them: the gender. My printed images were accepted, but I was still in suspense about my identification, which the school did not request from me until government officials were due to arrive for an inspection.

At my first job in Guangzhou, I had lied and said my identification card was lost. The manager of Ms. Wu's company hadn't said anything, but he had looked incredulous. Remembering that scene didn't feel good.

This time, I didn't want to lie or make anyone suspicious of me, so after great internal struggle, I decided to hand over my identification card and prepared for the worst. I gave it to the Vice-Principal, Ms. Lydia, in the morning and spent the whole day wondering when the judgment would come. When it did, would I be humiliated? Despised? Rejected? Fired?

But when Ms. Lydia returned my identification card at the end of the workday, she said nothing. I supposed she hadn't noticed the character on it that declared me female.

Many months later, the anomaly was discovered on the photocopy of my identification card. I was called to the office where Principal Maria and Ms. Lydia were waiting for me. At first I did not know why I had been summoned, but I heard, "Why is your ID female? Please explain and you can stay, otherwise, you must leave."

My face must have gone pale. I had known I could not escape this moment forever, but what could I say? For a long time I stood mute and they looked at me sternly. Finally, I uttered, "I'm transsexual."

The tension on their faces eased. Of course they were shocked, but they offered acceptance and compassion. Ms. Maria said the same thing Mr. Zhao had said to me, "Ok. Please don't tell anybody else. We will keep this secret for you."

What a relief. Given the great sum of money needed for surgery, it was unlikely I would be able to solve my identification card problems in the near future. But, Ms. Maria's acceptance of me meant that load was off my mind for the time being.

I felt like I had arrived at some sort of paradise. All my colleagues were Christian, God's word was taught at the school every day, there were songs and instrumentals devoted to him, coworkers loved and respected each other, and the laughter of children surrounded us. At the school, people called me by my English name, Mr. Ray, which I enjoyed. It was as if the name Lei Jing had been buried; I was rarely reminded of it. Life was renewed. I rented a house on my own and traveled to work on foot instead of in a crowded bus. I had friends again and was able to live as my authentic self.

CHAPTER 20
My Fantastic Idea

My salary was still as low, sixteen hundred yuan monthly, so saving was little by little. I constantly calculated how much I could put away after a few months. As I rushed about in the scorching sun, putting up with the great uneasiness from my body, any hardship seemed worthwhile if I could reach my goal. So, I endured what I had to and, stumbling, managed to get through the first year in Guangzhou with a bit of money tucked away for top surgery.

Originally, I planned to go to Shanghai to have the surgery during winter vacation. There were two hospitals in Shanghai that did most top surgeries in China. On the Internet chat room, I had heard of a doctor called Lu who was qualified to diagnose gender dysphoria and give the necessary papers for the surgery. Altogether, including traveling fees, I estimated at least 12,000 yuan was required. Then, I got an idea that saved a lot of trouble and explanation. I could seek a diagnosis of "hyperplasia of male mammary glands."

On August 23rd, I posted a message on a website, which was a platform for plastic surgery hospitals and clinics. I asked for fees and left my phone number. Soon after, a phone call came in from the website, asking about my needs and recommending Boshi Hospital. In the following hours and days, texts and calls from different local hospitals came one after another. There was even a call from Doctor Dai of another hospital asking for my QQ account, which would allow them to contact me through email and instant message. Some sent their address, asking me to come in for a consult. The price Boshi quoted was 8 to 10 thousand and the other hospital was asking 10 to 12 thousand. I was amazed at the power of money. It was like a magnet, drawing people in. As Ecclesiastes says, money is the answer for everything. But, Ms. Wu had not paid me yet, so I had to wait.

For the next month, I was filled with joy and excitement over my fantastic idea. There was anxiety too, because the chances of slipping up were large, but as soon as the money was ready, I could go to consult as a patient of hyperplasia of male mammary glands.

In the last third of September, Ms. Wu handed me my salary, two thousand yuan, and had a relaxed conversation with me in her house. As she chatted, my mind was already flying to the ATM, putting the cash in my account, and seeing the sum seven thousand eight hundred yuan displayed on the screen. With that, plus the several hundred I had stashed in a drawer at home, and my slightly higher wage, which had been raised to eighteen hundred yuan a month, I could not only see the shadow, but the silhouette of my wish. I could almost touch it.

Not long after that, I got a text message from a hospital saying plastic surgeries were on 50% off special for the 17th anniversary of the hospital during National Day. There are seven days off during National Day from October 1st to 7th. It is a very busy season and there are usually discounts for all kinds of consumption.

So, on Saturday, September 24th, I nervously made a call to Dr. Dai. A kind, sweet voice answered the phone. She told me this kind of surgery was not included in the special offer, but because of National Day there should be some favorable terms. I asked if I could consult that day, she said, "Of course," and sent me the address and appointed time.

Then, I specially washed my favorite white shirt. As soon as it was dry that afternoon, I put it on and set out. I wanted to leave a good impression on the doctor to show I was a *normal* male by appearance when wearing a shirt, even though there was the problem of *hyperplasia of male mammary glands*.

The hospital was located in one of the busiest districts of Guangzhou. I successfully found it by the signs in the subway station and the distinguished crimson building of the cosmetology department that stood near the street.

Inside, I was greeted by one of the receptionists, decorous and nice young ladies in light pink uniforms. The receptionist led me to a rest area filled with red chairs and sofas, poured me a cup of water, and told me to wait. As I settled into a chair, my tension was allayed somehow. The reception hall was wide, shiny, and magnificently decorated. For the first time, I noticed that my faithful canvas bag, which had followed me for four years, looked old and improper in that grand environment. On the wall opposite was a display introducing some of the doctors. Below that was a large, long aquarium that looked like a wall of fish. On the right side of the aquarium, various certificates hung. Some were copper etched and given from America. Left of the aquarium was a corridor with small rooms on each side. Above each door hung a little rectangular sign that said, "Office of Doctor. . ." Clients went in and out occasionally. There were some magazines issued by the hospital on the tea cart next to me. I picked one up and browsed the cases publicized inside. It seemed to be quite a credible hospital, or perhaps I was just trying to persuade myself I had made the right decision.

There was also a girl waiting. She sat across from me, looking thin and blue, and had a slightly artistic temperament. A receptionist holding a clipboard and pen came and asked for her registration information. "How old are you?"

"Eighteen," the girl said, mature beyond the age revealed by her voice.

I am old, and yet I appear to be twenty, I thought to myself. I hate that I look so improperly young. People don't respect me as my age deserves.

I did not think the girl needed any plastic surgery, in the same way nobody would ever think I needed it when I walked through a crowd. Spots, scars, and defects, if there are any, may only be apparent and magnified in one's own heart. Who would think I had this great secret hidden, torturing me year after year? How ironic that my breasts existed as a sign of healthiness, as necessary parts of a female body. Who would not love and care for his body? But there I was, eager to get rid of them via surgical knives.

After a while, I was summoned to Doctor Feng's office, which was the second door on the left of the corridor. I learned Doctor Dai, whom I had expected to meet, was only the assistant to Doctor Feng. Upon opening the door, I was greeted by a lady in her thirties sitting behind a desk. She wore a fine pair of glasses and her hair was in a bun. She looked thin and nimble, spoke fast and straight. Though she was in a white gown, I felt she was more like an experienced senior saleslady. I could sense her sincerity, but could not tell if it was genuine.

I sat down opposite her by the desk and unbuttoned my shirt to show her. She said the surgery fee was ten to fifteen thousand yuan. I said frankly, "I can only afford eight thousand."

She accepted the eight thousand too readily for my comfort. But, she explained, the fee for general anesthesia was an additional one thousand yuan. Partial anesthesia was free. Obviously, my money was not enough to afford general anesthesia.

"How long does it hurt with the partial anesthesia?" I asked.

"About ten minutes."

Having no concept of what surgery entailed, I believed she meant I would actually feel the knives cutting through my skin. I feared I would not be able to bear it. I lowered my head, struggling greatly; my hands felt so wet and cold. Finally, I said, "Sorry, I can't make a decision now. Let me go back and consider this, I will give you an answer tomorrow."

I figured I would comparison shop Baoshi hospital in the meantime, but Doctor Feng was not about to give me a chance to slip away.

"What are you considering? The anesthesia?"

"Yes."

"Let's do this. I will apply for you to have the general anesthesia free. Our president happens to be here today. I just need his signature." She rose and went out.

Now I was left alone in that small room. It was so quiet I could hear my heart racing. My brain was worrying about the decision ahead of me. If the anesthesia could be free, then my savings would be enough. I could proceed. But what if the price at the other hospital was cheaper? Those savings were, after all, my blood and sweat! But if this hospital waived the fee for anesthesia, that would be a bonus. There wasn't much time, so I resorted to a simple prayer, asking God to help me make the right decision.

The door opened behind me and Doctor Feng blew in like the wind. "The anesthesia will be free," she announced. She said I did not even need to fill out an application, she would write it up for me. Then she handed me a form that asked for my personal information: name, identification number, address, etc. Except name, I filled in everything truthfully. Immediately, she input my information into the computer on her desk and then passed me a VIP card. "We just have one condition. We will take a picture of your symptoms to keep for a case study, okay?" Clearly she had assumed my agreement before asking me, so she continued without waiting for a reply. "A medical examination must be performed to see if you are suitable for surgery. Have the examination today, okay? The results come in half an hour." The total fees for surgery, examination, admission, and medication were about 9,000 yuan.

Inevitably, she asked me why I hadn't had surgery earlier. I made up a story, telling her my family lived in the countryside and were too poor to send me to hospital so I hadn't been able to come until I could save the money. She asked when and how the condition had developed. I lied, telling her "since adolescence" and "due to an endocrine disorder." Fortunately, she did not dig too deeply into my case, nor did she suspect I was transsexual. Her focus was solving the problem and winning every client she could. I guessed it was out of curiosity she asked about my genitals. "It's. . .very small," I lied, timidly.

Her voice took on a tone of comforting sympathy. "You don't have a girlfriend, do you? We can't help with your genitals, but you may visit an andrology hospital. The breast surgery we can help with. Don't worry. We have had some cases like yours, including sex change cases."

With that, Dr. Feng turned me over to a receptionist—also called a guide—who accompanied me to each section of the required examination. It was like an adventure. I was curious, and also worried about whether or not my gender would accidentally show up on some test. There was a blood test and urine test, an electrocardiogram, and Doppler ultrasound, where I lay on a couch with my shirt open and pipes all around me. Something that felt cool was rubbed back and forth on my breasts. I heard the doctor say to her partner, "A kind of hyperplasia."

The thickness of my breasts was measured as 0.7 inches and 0.6 inches, and the official diagnosis was "mammary gland disorder," which proved the illness, making it reasonable and imperative I have the operation. With the medical examination finished and the results declared normal, I felt relieved, because there was no room for me to waver any more. Doctor Feng recommended me to Doctor Li and arranged the surgery for the next Thursday morning. I prepaid four thousand yuan and left.

It had been such a long day. Dusk fell and neon lights popped on. Joyous and relieved, I drifted with the crowd, in the dim light of evening, down a busy street near the hospital. I did not feel like going home, so I wandered to a square where I stood in a corner out of the breeze and casually watched passersby.

It dawned on me it was September 24th. On the same date, two years before, I had been carried to a prison in the suburb of Beijing, forced to undergo a physical examination, then carried a transparent plastic cup of my urine within the sight of many people so it could be tested. I had just had the same experience in a different place, a southern city, except I paid for it. The day of my surgery, September 29th, was the same date I had been released from detention. What a coincidence. September 24 and September 29 seemed to be significant dates for me.

I thought I would be very excited when my dream for more than a decade was finally going to become true, but after so much struggling, wanting, frustration, and desperation, I felt only peace. In a few days, the bulges on my chest would be no more. They were part of my body, legally existed, but brought me so much uneasiness. Now they were finally to depart and disturb me no more.

My phone rang. It was my sister Yun. We talked about how amazed we were that it had been such a long time since we had seen each other, but by no means could I tell her about what had just happened and what was going to happen to me. I had no intention of telling anybody, or rather, there was nobody I could tell, not even my closest family. Who would share this joy with me? Who would really feel happy for me? People would only shake their heads and believe I had gone insane.

CHAPTER 21

Top Surgery

Monday, Tuesday, Wednesday...I counted each day with anticipation. I had to tell Ms. Maria, in advance, that I needed two days off: Thursday and Friday. So, at the end of the workday on Wednesday, I went to her office. We talked briefly about my work and she expressed her approval of the job I was doing, promising to raise my salary in three months, depending on my performance.

Finally she asked, "Are you traveling?"

I hadn't planned to tell anybody about my surgery, but I replied to her question without thinking. Perhaps I subconsciously wanted someone to know and felt she was the one I could tell.

"No, but I'm going to have an operation tomorrow morning to have my breasts removed," I said lightly.

She looked pale suddenly. She could not say anything for a while. When she did speak, softly and slowly, there was worry, sorrow, sympathy and love, in her voice.

"Did you pray?" she asked. "Are you at peace?"

"Yes."

"I am not trying to prevent you from doing this, but I hope you won't regret it, because this is irreversible." She began to cry.

Seeing those tears, knowing that at least someone acknowledged my affliction and sympathized with me—that a heart in this world stood with me when I was alone—I could not hold back anymore. I lowered my head and wept too.

Ms. Maria looked at me, eyes brimming with tears. "You are like my own son," she said. Every time I see you smile or see you cheer up, I feel happy for you. Do you know why? Because God loves you and I love you too." With a lump in her throat, she continued: "I was once rejected and unaccepted. I know how it feels. It was my Sunday School teacher who loved me. If you like, you can take me as your spiritual mother."

Whenever I recall this scene, warmth and gratitude overwhelm me. Ms. Maria touched me deeply.

Doctor Feng had been thoughtful and made good arrangements for me. She said it would be hectic during National Day, so she scheduled my surgery for the twenty ninth to avoid the crowds. She also made sure my operation was the first one of the morning. She said the surgeons usually worked well in the morning, when they were freshest. She even called me the day before to remind me: "Arrive at the hospital on time at 8:30. Don't drink or eat anything that morning. Wear a dark shirt, or it will look obvious and strange when you leave the hospital."

The night before my surgery, I went shopping, stored food, tidied up my room, took a bath and did some washing, knowing I would not be able to manage these tasks for a few days after the operation. At one o'clock, when everything was silent and everybody else was asleep, the light in my house was still on. I took farewell pictures of my breasts, then drank some water and went to bed. I lay very still, but I could not fall asleep all night. I was too nervous and excited.

September 29, 2011, I rose and, on the doctor's suggestion, put on a plain black t-shirt. It was the only t-shirt in my wardrobe. As was my habit, I added an extra layer: a short-sleeved gray shirt. I arrived at the hospital earlier than 8:30 am. The receptionists hadn't even put on their uniforms yet, neither was Doctor Feng in her white garment. Without her lab coat, she was an elegant woman dressed in beautiful fitting clothing, high-heeled shoes, and a spiffy bun. I filled out an emergency contact form in her office and then was led to the second floor to have my picture taken and pay the rest of the fees. Then, I was handed over to a guide, and I have never seen Doctor Feng since.

The guide took me to another floor. I wasn't sure which one. I sat facing a long, wide corridor that was clean and filled with bright ceiling lights. Nurses like busy bees went in and out of the wards on both sides. I studied the corridor while someone took my blood pressure and temperature. I wanted to engrave the scene on my memory because finally, finally, I was in the waiting room of a substantial, capable hospital and about to have an operation I had dreamed of day and night.

"It's for you from the hospital," said a young man in a white garment as he placed a box of milk on the glass teapoy in front of me. The young man checked my medical examination report.

Next, a genial middle-aged doctor arrived. He also checked the report, and then asked me questions: "Have you ever had surgery before? Do you smoke or drink alcohol? Any allergies? Any history of diabetes in your family?" Simultaneously, he made swift notes, then I was required to sign a paper. Afterward, I learned the young doctor was the surgeon's assistant. The older one was the anesthetist, who was a chief.

A pink plastic bracelet specifying my ward information was placed on my wrist so they would know where to put me after the surgery. Then I was taken to a ward on the left side of the corridor, given a patient suit, which looked like fat pink pajamas, and told to put them on without underpants. I wondered why I wasn't to wear underpants, but I did what I was told in the bathroom and stowed my bag in a locker. I had to tie the locker key to my ward bracelet.

I sat on the bed for a while. A nurse came in. It turned out I had a mild fever, so she gave me an injection in my hip. She hung a bottle of NaCI on a rack and pierced a vessel on my left hand with a needle. I had never had an IV drip before. The back of my hand felt cool from the transparent liquid being dripped into it. When the IV bottle was about half empty, a couple of female assistants about my age arrived. They were wearing dark green doctor's overalls and masks. Together, they walked me and my IV bottle through the corridor to the elevator, where one of them kindly asked if I felt nervous.

"Yes," I said.

"Of course you are," she replied. "Take it easy, it is only a simple surgery." Then she asked, in a friendly way, "Where is your hometown?" I told her, and though I could only see her eyes above the surgical mask she was wearing, her look was so sincere and concerned that I was comforted.

We traveled to another floor, again I did not know which one; then, we turned right out of the elevator and walked to the end of the corridor where the operating rooms were located. I had to change into a fresh set of slippers before I was allowed in.

I hadn't expected the operating room to be so large, wide and empty. The temperature was so cold in there, I could not help trembling. The operating table was narrow and covered with something that had the texture of leather. I was to lay on it, shirtless. A light blue cap was put on my head. A heavy, army-green quilt was placed over my lower body and my upper garment was spread across the quilt.

The surgeon appeared. He was a vigorous, middle-aged man with dark, broad eyebrows who spoke loudly. He had me sit up and drew two big circles around each of my breasts with a marker.

"Young man, your nipples are too big. What shall I do? I can only help you take out the gland. I'll make it minimally invasive to reduce scarring, though your money isn't actually enough to pay for that."

Next, I had to lay down with my arms stretched out and fastened as if I was being nailed to a cross. The anesthetist, Chief Liu, came in carrying a syringe. It was the biggest syringe I'd ever seen. It was about one-third full of medical liquid and had a frighteningly long needle. I raised my head to watch as yellow iodine was spread liberally across my chest.

"Don't look!" Chief Liu said. He ordered a piece of canvas be set before me to block my view. The staff was visiting casually, someone asked someone else if she had had breakfast yet. The atmosphere was light and friendly.

Chief Liu started to give me injections around my breasts. Automatically, my right shoulder raised up against the pain, but he pushed it back down.

I had expected to fall asleep and be aware of nothing, but I was conscious from beginning to end, though in a kind of half narcosis. I heard them talking and Doctor Li, the surgeon, asked an assistant to bring something for the liposuction, but also, scenes of working at school haunted my head and the sound of children echoed in my ears. My breathing was smooth, as if I was sleeping, but not actually sleeping. I felt no pain, but something was poking violently inside my flesh with such force my body was almost pulled off the table. That explained why they had fastened me down. Then there was the sound of scissors cutting. Before long, the right side was done, then the left. Upon finishing his part, the surgeon left the suturing to his assistant and departed. The stitching process was slow. I could see the doctor's sleeve move back and forth in the air beyond the canvas.

Another assistant held out a steel tray for me to see and said, "These are the glands that were cut out." There was a lump of something fleshy in the tray.

"So much," I said, weakly.

The assistant said she was going to dump them.

"Yes, please," I said.

After I was stitched up, they put a large napkin over my wounds and lapped bandages tightly around my chest. Then they became serious and strained. Cooperating, orderly, they shifted me to a stretcher. One held the IV bottle, some pushed the stretcher, and we were soon out of the operating room. Bright lights on the ceiling flashed by and then their rhythm would be interrupted when my light blue cap slid over my eyes. A hand helped me reposition it from time to time. Into the elevator and out to the ward and finally I was shifted to my bed. According to the nurse's instructions, I must lay still, without a pillow, for a few hours.

At some point, another male patient was brought to share the ward with me. He was accompanied by a woman. They did not talk very much, but kept the television on until late into the night. For the first time in my life, the noise of the television was unbearable to me, although it was not very loud. I had never had such a great longing for quiet, but I did not want to bother the couple about watching television. After all, it was not my own room.

As the day wore on, my body became so feeble I barely had strength to speak. I was thirsty and wished I could sleep through some of those terrible hours, but never lost consciousness. The IV kept dripping, one bottle after another, until 7:30 p.m. A nurse came in once in a while to manage the IV or take my temperature and blood pressure. Though my back felt tired from hours of lying still, I hardly felt my wounds. Maybe the anesthesia was still controlling my pain. I moved my legs and hips to give my back some relief. Sometimes I gazed at the liquid medicine dripping from the IV bottle, drop by drop, like the rain I used to watch falling from the eaves during my childhood. Most of the time, however, my eyes were closed, and the kids at school were flashing through my mind.

I had a wonderful nurse that day. Her attentive care warmed me so much that I am motivated to love the people around me whenever I remember her. I should have asked her name, but didn't think of it. I did keep a note she wrote me in my journal as a keepsake of how kindly I was treated by a stranger when I was sick.

Maybe she saw I was young and alone and that roused her tenderness, though I might have been older than her. I was happy every time she walked into the room and she seemed happy to see me, too. By comparison, the nurse attending the other patient was rather indifferent and spoke to him coldly. As my nurse was giving me her attention, I realized it had been a long time since I had been cared for like this.

Seeing my garment had slipped, my nurse pulled it back over me lest I catch a cold and asked with concern, "Does the wound hurt?"

"Not much," I muttered.

She scrutinized me. "You didn't sleep well last night, did you? Your eyes are bloodshot."

I thought that was so sweet of her, for who would bother to notice my eyes?

"Please avoid eating beef, mutton, strong coffee or tea after surgery," she reminded me, kindly.

"No beef?" I asked, thinking of the beef jerky I had stored for meals.

"Why? You like beef?" she asked with a smile. "Your lips are so dry. Shall I take a cotton swab and dip it in water to wet your lips?"

So, she wetted my lips. Her thoughtfulness and the way she looked at me reminded me of a loving wife. Such intimacy seemed impossible for a man and a woman who were not lovers. Here we were, strangers, yet she demonstrated her care spontaneously and purely. Was it because she was a nurse and I was her patient? Or did she feel some personal affection for me?

I was allowed some fruit six hours after the anesthetic was estimated to have worn off. I ate two cherry tomatoes and immediately suspected the anesthesia was still in effect, because I ended up with horrible nausea for the next few hours. I became extremely pale and sick to my stomach. After finally throwing up the last green bile, I fell asleep. When I woke at some hour after midnight, the ward was dark. My roommate and his wife were sharing one bed and snoring soundly. I could hear rain pattering outside. Was it raining for me? It reminded me of Ms. Maria's tears, which made my own eyes wet.

"You look much better today," my nurse said with a smile the next morning. I was glad to see her and grateful my nausea had passed. I was able to sit up and walk, though not as vigorously as usual, after breakfast.

"Your temperature is normal now. You had a little fever yesterday," my nurse commented after taking my vital signs. She also told me there were just a few more IV bottles to drip today.

To my surprise, another nurse brought a big bunch of carnations and put them on the bedside table.

"From the hospital," she explained, "wishing you a quick recovery."

I looked and looked at those red carnations—the first bunch of flowers I had ever received—fresh and flourishing with dew on the petals. They brought me delight. Alas, I was unable to carry them home. My bag was burden enough for me. I had packed it with a book and toiletries, naively thinking I would be able to read and wash.

In the afternoon, when I was supposed to leave the hospital, I removed the patient suit and changed back into my clothes. I looked in the mirror. My hair was messy, my face felt oily and had a little beard, but my chest was very flat under the t-shirt. Even the bandage was inconspicuous, though it squeezed my chest so tightly, it was exhausting. It forced my shoulders up, bent my neck and back forward, and prevented me from raising my arms completely.

I went straight to a restaurant near the hospital. Pushing open the heavy door required great effort due to my bindings, but I made it and took a seat by a French window. After a slow and proper meal, I lingered to watch the passersby. From inside the restaurant, it was like watching pantomime: much activity, but no sound. My solitude, separate from the background noise of the world, eased something inside me.

I reckoned I could take a bus home, since it would cost too much to take a taxi so far. The money I had left needed to tide me over for a month. My plan was to go to a bus terminal two metro stops away. I moved among the rushing crowd in the subway with the speed of a turtle, fearing someone would bump into me. Luck was with me, and I caught a direct bus.

Night fell and the atmosphere of National Day was in the air. The bus ran peacefully through the city past buildings, roads and bridges. The passengers were subdued; each seemed to be in his or her own world. It was only another ordinary Friday to most. I was watching the city outside the window. It looked serene and safe. Lights decorated the sky. "Goodbye, my last hurting summer," I said to myself. Next time the heat descended, I would be prepared for it.

As I was exiting the bus, my phone rang. It was Miss H., a colleague from the school.

"Ray, I heard you had an operation, what happened? Are you OK?"

I wondered how she knew; her kind regard caught me unprepared.

"Er. . .I. . .I got a fever," I replied.

"A fever?" she asked incredulously. "What on Earth happened?"

"Nothing, I'm fine, just a cold." I was frantically searching for words, but trying to keep my voice calm.

Miss H. persisted in questioning me, but failed to get any more information, and so my health issues remained a mystery to her.

Another colleague, Miss W., called the moment I sat down in my chair at home. She said she was passing by my house and would like to visit me. She had heard I had an operation. In the yellow lamp light of my room, she encouraged me to share my hardships with her. She recognized I must be facing some difficulties, but could not tell what they were. I sat stiffly, sore from my wounds and exhausted by the pressing of the bandage, and responded primarily with silence while she talked.

Finally, I asked, "How did you know I had an operation?"

"Ms. Maria mentioned it in her prayer at the close of the staff meeting."

"Why did she mention this?" I asked with a frown.

Seeing my sullenness, Miss W. said gently, "She meant no harm."

Perhaps Miss W. touched her own heart as she was comforting me. She cried. I was moved too, and struggling over whether or not to tell her the truth, though I appeared to be staring blankly at the floor. A great tide of emotion was rising and falling within me.

"I. . ." the tide rose, and I felt an impulse to lift my shirt and tell her everything. "No! Don't tell!" some internal power hissed inside my head. The tide faded and silence was my only reply to her questions. There were things not to be shared. It was too risky.

"You have many qualities that girls like," Miss W. said. "You are gentle, thoughtful, talented, charming ... why are you unhappy? God really loves you. You are precious and honored in his eyes."

"Is it God that sent you to tell me he loves me?" I asked. For a long time, I had not been sure if what I did pleased him or if what I did was a sin against him.

"Maybe," said Miss W. Then we were silent together.

After she left, I lay down immediately. I spent most of the following days in bed.

On October 2nd, I returned to the hospital to have my bandages changed and stitches removed. There was a scar about one and a half inches long under each armpit. On October 8th, I returned to work. Nobody there perceived anything different about me and life went on as usual.

There were still times when I felt depressed and lonely, but with this trouble removed, a burden was released. I was relieved, relaxed and confident wherever I went and whatever I did. I still stooped out of habit, but now that I could stand up straight and bold, I practiced better posture, reminding myself the breasts were no more.

CHAPTER 22

Maximized Manhood

About two months after my top surgery, I attended "Maximized Manhood," which had been recommended by Ms. Maria. Maximized Manhood was a series of courses held during a three-day retreat that taught Biblical perspectives on the role of men. Ms. Maria's suggestion I attend this retreat told me that she not only accepted me, but also encouraged me to embrace my authentic self, or as she said, "learn to be a man."

After one section of the courses, there was a prayer time. Everyone was standing before the dais. Some people prayed by themselves and some had a mentor at their side. I was content to stand a little ways away. I had finished my silent prayer and was watching the crowd when, out of the corner of my eye, I saw someone approaching. I turned and discovered it was one of the Indonesian teachers. I didn't know him. I had only been an audience member when he was speaking from the dais. Why was he coming toward me among hundreds of other people? His eyes were straight on me. They were sorrowful, deep eyes. To me, he seemed like a man who had undergone grief and thus could comprehend the despair of others.

His godliness was impressive, though his clothes were a bit

shabby. He stood in front of me, looked at me from head to foot, and gesticulated.

"Don't look at your body, look at your heart," he said.

Certainly, I knew what he was saying, but how was the very secret I was afraid to bring to light so transparent to this stranger? We had never met before. How had he discovered this knowledge about me? I could only attribute it to God's revelation.

"Just accept yourself," he continued, looking at me intently. Then he pointed at me and said, "Jesus loves you. Jesus loves you. Always remember Jesus loves you!"

For a moment, we stood still, facing each other. I explained nothing and he understood everything. Finally, I walked up and held him and he held me too.

It was not the first time I had heard, "accept yourself," but what did it mean when it was said to me in this special circumstance? Maybe I had not really been accepting myself, for I was expecting perfection that would never happen in this lifetime. I was rejecting defects. I had accepted the person I was inside, but not my body the way it was born. There had always been a split between the two, and I had always suffered over the disagreement between my body and soul. Considering the stranger's words, I came to believe they meant it was time for me to accept my transgender identity: accept both body and soul as part of myself, accept my existence in its unique form, accept being transsexual as a gift.

I had been doubting God's love and shaming myself over it. There was always a voice in my head accusing me of not accepting the body he created for me and insisting on my own way. Now, God confirmed his love through his servant. From then on, when I had doubts or heard condemnation from other Christians, I recalled my baptism by Mr. Zhao and the confirmation of God's love and acceptance by this Indonesian teacher. I am resolved to keep my faith between myself and God. As it says in Romans 14:22 (NIV): "Blessed is the one who does not condemn himself by what he approves."

One session of Maximized Manhood dealt with bitterness over fathers or original families. We all gathered at the front of the room where the Indonesian teacher stood on the dais.

With deep emotion and regret he said, "Everybody, please look at me. Here, may I represent your father to apologize to you. I am sorry. I don't know how to be a father. I am not a good father. I ask for your forgiveness. Please, forgive me."

The trainees were all single young men and some sobbed as the teacher delivered these words. The sincere apology softened all our hearts. Although we might never hear an apology from the people who actually hurt us, when we forgave, we were released.

Memories of my father rose in my mind and tears welled up in my eyes. My father had not seen me. He passed by when I was bullied. When I injured my wrist, there was no care, only a torrent of abuse. After I fell into an ice cave and was lying on the kang alone, calling for someone to come to me, he did not respond. No one came at all. I was dispensable in the family and never treasured. The sufferings of my childhood were terrible to recall. They overwhelmed me like dark clouds and weighed me down. I could not deceive myself that nothing had happened. The old hurts lurked and jumped out, time and again, to block me, pull me, prevent me from going on my way. I had to face them and have them dealt with; forgiveness was the only way out.

Forgiveness, as we are instructed in Romans 12:19 is giving up the thought of a right to avenge, knowing vengeance is the Lord's; he will repay. To forgive is to say to debtors, "You don't owe me anymore," and cross out your record of their wrongs. I had a decision to forgive, and I had a need to forgive, but I did not forgive all at once. I made efforts. I struggled. Haunted by my dark memories over and over, I prayed. With the help of the Holy Spirit, I made it, but I had dreams for a long time after I forgave.

In one dream, I was at home. I opened a door. Wide empty space came into view. Colors met my eye from everywhere. Paintings, framed and glazed, were hanging in orderly fashion on all the walls. I moved close to each one in turn, looking at them carefully. I was surprised to recognize they were all my works. In this dream, I could not help but smile and feel touched, for Dad had collected all my works and saved them, secretly, in a special room. He treasured this art because it was the work of his son, even though the paintings were simple and naive. In another dream, I was a child, walking with

Dad along the riverbank on the road to the primary school. We were communing with each other as we strolled.

In real life, there was little sign he was proud of me. There was no communion, no time spent especially with me, except for the day he taught me to ride a motorcycle. I had to accept the earthly paternity that I dreamed of would always only be fantasy. It was my heavenly Father who held me when I failed and cheered when I made progress. All I could do was set my relationship with him above all relations on Earth and forgive the rest.

Since moving to Guangzhou, I had acquired the space to breathe, to rest, to reflect, and to grow. I had experienced healing and been restored through my work at the school, my new church, and fellowship with brothers and sisters. Meanwhile, I was aware my parents were getting older and the only child still left at home was Boy. When I spoke to my parents by phone, I sensed they had started to miss their children. Eventually, I wanted to see them too. In the summer of 2012, I decided to visit my home town.

By this time, China had passed a law requiring identification to purchase a train ticket. I would also have to show my identification card and ticket before boarding. I was self-conscious and leery, but I managed to buy a ticket. Then came the ticket collection line and, finally, the security line. To my relief, there were so many people filing onto the train, the ticket collector barely noticed me or my credentials.

I took the train as far as possible and then transferred to a bus. The closer I got to my hometown, the more nervous I became. I was returning to the place I came from, where my history and background resided. I knew when I got off that bus I would have to confront my memories.

I got off the bus and walked toward my childhood home. As I crossed the bridge, I saw my mother standing in the road. She had abandoned her ironing to watch for my return.

Mom did not recognize me until I was close enough she could see my smile. Then she smiled back and said, "I was thinking, who is this young man?"

Though my parents continued to refer to me as their daughter or my siblings' sister, they did not scold or criticize me for how I dressed. I was not a child anymore, after all. I had been worried they would ask about my missing breasts, but they didn't notice, or if they did, they said nothing. They never asked how or why I appeared so different.

Some of the neighbors did not recognize me either. If they dropped in to borrow or bring something, inevitably they would ask if I was a son-in-law or wonder aloud if my father had one son or two. My parents never failed to shock them by introducing me as their daughter.

I heard from Mom that the neighbor boy had prospered, owned more than one house in the county, and his family had moved to Australia so his son could study there. At first I was surprised about this news, but then recalled Psalm 73:12 (NIV), "This is what the wicked are like—always free of care, they go on amassing wealth."

I did not let it bother me, but took comfort in Psalm 37:1-2 (NIV): "Do not fret because of those who are evil or be envious of those who do wrong; for like the grass they will soon wither, like green plants they will soon die away."

Boy had not prospered. Years of sunburn and dirtiness had given him a very dark complexion. He was diminished and bony, his cheeks sunken and the shape of his skull clearly visible. His head was shaved like a prisoner's, his forehead was wrinkled, there was a sparse mustache on his upper lip. He resembled a little old man, but his mind was still childish and perverted. He often put on a police uniform someone had given him and limped about the town. Sometimes he fished in the river, and he collected scrap and made a little money from it.

Boy didn't recognize me at first and asked himself who I was. Later, he learned who I was, but didn't say much. He seldom spoke to other family members, but if he was spoken to, he replied.

One day, I reached to the rusty handle that opened the door to Boy's room. As I pushed it open, a pungent sickening odor blew out. The windows were dusty, the walls and ceiling grayed from smoke. There were cobwebs in the corners. Worn out, muddy shoes, socks, and fishing nets, were piled among heaps of rubbish and scraps that

Boy collected. His quilt was a stained rag, loosely rolled up. Dirty clothes that must have been accumulating for years and two chests on the kang formed a dump heap that left very little space for him to sleep. This was the very kang I had trampled madly to vent my anger as a child. I had an apple in one hand. I placed it on the kang and was turning to leave when I spotted a note on the wall. The squiggle on it was Boy's. It said, "Christ Jesus came into the world to save sinners." I cannot describe how I felt seeing those powerful words of truth in that place. Mom said Boy went to the local church, but who knows if he really understood the Gospel or believed Jesus?

During dinner one night, I asked Boy if he went to church or knew any praise songs. He retrieved an old song book from his room and passed it to me. Pointing at a well-known song, I asked Boy if he could sing. He shook his head no.

When the Scripture says, "Do not hate your brother in your heart; do not seek revenge, but love your neighbor as yourself," I think of this visit and everything I saw. I believe if Boy had been brought up with love and care, things might have been different with him. I felt sorry for him. He had needed good parents, too.

Subsequent visits home were easier. My parents have never accepted me as a son, but they have accepted how I am. They comment on my appearance, saying I am thin and dark, remarking at how my Adam's apple protrudes, or pointing out I have more leg hair than my father. Suspecting I was using hormones, they once asked me about it, but I did not give a straight answer and they did not press the matter. To avoid looking too conspicuous, I shave my beard when I visit them.

The hardest issue is being referred to as a woman while I am there. Once, I visited my Mom's shop in town. As I had expected, one of the guests asked about me and Mom introduced me as her daughter. The guest was startled and began watching whatever I did. Feeling those eyes upon me, I was very embarrassed.

My parents do not understand my distress over being identified as a woman. At first, I hoped to alter the way they talk about me, but I no longer expect that will happen. I have been watching them as closely as they have been watching me and come to realize that, like me, they are just the people they are. Mom and Dad are also subject to their inborn traits, experiences, education and time. Like me, they are victims of their original families, not treasured by their own parents.

As a child, I could not understand why they were not like the doting parents of my peers. As a man, I know they are just not expressive people. They don't know how to say they love me directly. They do not hug or touch affectionately. But, they have their own ways of demonstrating their feelings for me. When I visit, they cook and offer me food. They are pleased to have me visit their work, and when it is time for me to return to Guangzhou, I can tell they wish I would stay longer. During phone calls, I can sense they hope to see me again soon and are concerned for my well-being. They always ask if I have enough money. I never ask for any, but I know if I did, they would transfer funds into my account.

Mom and Dad have probably always had their own ways of expressing their love; I just needed to learn that. I think particularly of how they supported me going to university despite having a big family and a lot of expenses.

It requires a strong mindset to keep my peace when my parents call me their daughter, especially in front of strangers, but I have learned to forgive them and try to understand. To see the love they are able to give and appreciate it. To accept them for who they are in the same way I wish to be accepted for who I am.

CHAPTER 23
Miracles

In the heat and humidity of my home in southern China, I missed the north: the cool summer breezes, the clear autumn sky, the pure winter snow. I had been fantasizing about swimming in the northern rivers, shirtless, happy, and free, like a creature born to live in the water. I often imagined myself standing on the stone bridge, diving in a para-curve into a river that ran along the feet of verdant mountains. In Guangzhou, while the noise of motorbikes rushed by my window and the fan blew hot air onto my body, I had dreams of swimming from island to island and lying under the water with the fish all around me for company. Then, I would awaken and find I was still in my bed in a foreign, subtropical city where most of the year is summer and temperatures are continually 34 C or higher.

One Sunday, I was sitting in the conference room at my church. Three air conditioners were running, so I had taken refuge from the terrible heat there. It was after service. Children were playing and adults were visiting, but I had no intention of talking to anyone. A couple of young men came and sat around me. One of them, obviously expecting me to say yes, said, "Brother, do you have time this afternoon? Let's go swimming!"

I wanted to go, but I couldn't. Public swimming pools are

forbidden places for me because they require me to expose my body, which I do not want to be judged by. I am aware my underpants will look suspiciously empty, my nipples abnormally big and dark compared to other men's, and I have scars by my armpits from top surgery. So, I made an excuse. "Sorry, I need to do some packing and cleaning before I leave to visit my parents the day after tomorrow. You guys have fun!"

When I returned to my hometown, swimming in the river as I had during my childhood was a joy I intended to savor. I originally planned to swim in the moonlight so nobody would see me. I once did that during a summer vacation from high school, which was my last memory of swimming. But one day, as I walked along the river levee, I discovered a perfect place for me to swim, hidden behind a corn field on the bank. At that spot, I could see cobbles on the riverbed, but the water did not look deep or dangerous, and few people went there.

On a fair July afternoon, I set out from home, walked to the end of the bridge, and turned right onto a narrow winding path that led down to the levee. A vast corn field was on the right side of the path, tossing in the wind like the waves of an endless green sea. On the left side of the path was the river. On that side, too, a dense hedge of corn grew, guarded by tall poplars.

The path wound through the rustling green, then arrived at a weedy clearing at the river's edge. I felt relieved and safe in this solitary domain where the water flowed east to west and there was nothing but nature for company. Ducks floating by the opposite bank broke the silence with their quacking. In the distance I could see the bridge, newly painted white. Cars passing over it looked like moving dots of different sizes. Here there were no more judging eyes, no more social identities.

I stripped off my shirt and shorts recklessly. It was the first time in my adulthood I had stood shirtless in the open air naturally and comfortably. I stepped into the river, still wearing my sandals, and walked west. The sun made silver flashes across the water. I bent and scooped handfuls of it into the air to see it fall like transparent pearls. I burst into laughter and tears. How I had missed the days when I was little, bathing in the river with my fellows all summer, catching fish, playing games, innocent of gender issues, bodies revealing little difference between male and female. As I had grown, so many things had become unpractical. Regardless of how much I loved to strip to the waist and swim, I had to suppress the urge. But, thanks to top surgery and years on testosterone, I could finally face my body without tension or disgust.

It would be a lie to say I had no fear of swimming alone in that unfamiliar section of the river. Only a fool knows no fear when he is not sure of what lies beneath the surface of water. Would there be pits? Could I still swim well after so many years?

At first I could see the riverbed, but as I went deeper it became invisible and unpredictable. I stepped forward carefully and nervously. The water soaked my knees, then thighs, then waist. It felt strange, chilling and exciting. Finally, I steeled my mind, took a deep breath, threw myself forward into the water, and paddled with my arms and legs. How joyful and exciting to learn I could still swim.

Water patted my chin as I advanced with the current, staying close to the river bank. There was another shore ahead, a big pile of stones. As I approached it, the water became shallower, so I stood up and walked to shore, amazed I had gone so far. When I looked back, my red t-shirt was barely visible on the reeds at the bank where I had entered the water. I sprawled across the cobbles, which were warm from the sun. I used a large rock for a pillow and looked up at the blue sky. Bunches of clouds, white and soft like cotton, looked close enough to touch. I lay there for a long while, trying to appreciate all this with my senses, feeling happy, content and grateful. In harmony with nature, I forgot about my body. It's shape, tall or short, fat or thin, male or female, was no longer important.

Eventually, I had to swim back against the current. It was exhausting work, and I needed a break halfway, so I tried to stand, but my feet failed to touch the ground! Before I realized what was happening, water flooded into my throat and covered my head. The sound of it filled my ears. Panic seized me. My arms flapped madly and my legs kicked so desperately that one of my sandals fell off my foot. The instant I managed to reach the surface, I uttered a faint, "Help!" Then I was pulled down again. I rose and sank, rose and sank; I do not know how long it lasted. I was almost convinced my life was about to end.

Though I had once wished to die and had long believed I was not afraid of death, when it came to me without warning, my fear was great and I resisted. Thoughts raced through my mind. Oh, if I could be just like those ducks floating by! Ah, there is no one to help me. My parents will wonder where I went. Will someone find my body? "My times are in your hands." Will my life really end here I wondered. Wasn't there more for me to do? Potential unfulfilled? Could this really be my final hour?

Suddenly, my bare foot touched something soft, but solid. I couldn't believe it was the riverbed, but it was! That was sand I was feeling! I was no longer sinking. I pushed my other foot down. My mouth was just above the water, allowing me to cough and gasp air.

It took a while before I felt able to turn around and size up my position. To my astonishment, not far behind me was my sandal. It should have been carried away by the current, but there it was, just meters away, floating toward me slowly and calmly. It was inexplicable to me, but all I had to do was stretch out and grab it when it drifted close enough.

I once told my college friend, Xiowen, I did not believe in miracles. That's not true anymore. Miracles are everywhere. We are just too accustomed to miracles to see them. The universe is a miracle. Life is a miracle. That I survived, in every sense, is a miracle.

For most of my years, I wondered about my place in this world. How should I exist? I was restless and bitter because I disliked the conditions of my life. I wanted to be one of the "normal" majority. Being marginalized frightened me. I could not see that, just as I am, I occupy a unique position in this world. No one else has ever been me or ever will be me. I am irreplaceable.

Until I accepted myself as a transgender man, I thought I could not be content unless I achieved a "whole" life by marrying and having children. Now, I realize I don't have to be like everyone else to be happy. Each kind of life has its own wonder and also its own price to be paid. Although my life is not what I expected, I see now that it is a miracle. Every transition in my life has wrought an everyday miracle. It is by the grace of God that I am who I am, and his grace to me has not been without effect.

God did not prevent bad things from happening to me, and I have suffered long, troubled times. Now, I am able to console others using the comfort demonstrated to me by God. My wish is to be an oasis, refreshing those who are weary. To be a source of light to those in darkness. To give justice instead of demanding it for only myself. To be a loving person rather than bemoaning the lack of love in the world.

I have struggled with ingratitude, immaturity and entitlement to the point of complete exhaustion. I have believed myself a creation of God, yet unworthy of my own love and acceptance. For years, I rejected what I have, desperate for what can never be. Because I have stumbled down these hard roads, I have learned that being a man has nothing to do with my external shape.

When my body is no more, dust to dust, ashes to ashes, how can anyone judge whether my soul is male or female? 1 Samuel 16: 7 says people look at the outward appearance, but the Lord looks at the heart. Perhaps after we leave this temporal existence, there is no gender at all.

I won't pretend I have completely overcome my concerns about living in the body I was born with. There is a reason I have shared my story using a pseudonym, after all. Church plays a big role in my life. I have stood on the dais to lead Bible readings and make the opening prayer. Occasionally, I have had the honor of sharing messages. I was appointed group leader of the single brothers and have listened to them and prayed for them. On a short missionary trip, I had to bed-share with another male. There have been ladies showing interest in me and one older woman wanted me for a son-in-law. Many are keen to introduce me to my next girlfriend. I have successfully merged into society as a man, it seems, but I know all this is based on the premise that I am a cisgender man. My past and my wonderful name for girls are unknown to them. I dare not imagine what the consequences would be if they discovered I am transgender. I suspect they would be as shocked as if they found an alien disguised as a human hiding amongst them. They might not know how to treat me anymore or be angry that I "deceived" them. Some "kind" hearts might try to "cure" me. I am glad that no one sees the scars at my armpits or has x-ray eyes that can penetrate my pants.

Despite this, I am more at peace with myself every day. I know the man I am, and he lives, miraculously, beyond my body.

CPSIA information can be obtained
at www.ICGtesting.com
Printed in the USA
LVOW03s1704090517
533890LV00015B/319/P